RS AND THEIR WORK

SOBEL ARMSTRONG
General Editor

Caryl Churchill

Val Rylands

CARYL CHURCHILL

Caryl Churchill

Elaine Aston

Northcote House
in association with
The British Council

First published in 1997 by Northcote House Publishers Ltd, Plymbridge House, Estover Road, Plymouth PL6 7PY, United Kingdom.
Tel: +44 (01752) 202368 Fax: +44 (01752) 202330.

British Library Cataloguing-in-Publication Data
A catalogue record for this book is available from the British Library

ISBN 0-7463-0836-1

Typeset by PDQ Typesetting, Newcastle-under-Lyme
Printed and bound in the United Kingdom

for Ian,
Magdalene and Daniel

Contents

Acknowledgements

I should like to thank Methuen and Nick Hern Books, the publishers of Caryl Churchill's works, whose excellent editions I used in writing this study. Thanks also to Nick Hern and Guy Chapman who generously shared early information about the script and production details of *Hotel*. I appreciated and enjoyed the thoughts and company of Janelle Reinelt at the *Light Shining in Buckinghamshire* revival. Finally, of course, special thanks to Caryl Churchill without whose outstanding work in the theatre this volume would not have been possible.

Biographical Outline

1938	Churchill born in London. Early childhood spent in and near London, with exception of short time spent in Lake District during war years.
1948	Just before age of 10, family move to Canada and live in Montreal until Churchill nearly 17.
1957–60	Student years at Lady Margaret Hall, Oxford. Student productions of *Downstairs* (1958), which went to NUS festival, and *Having a Wonderful Time* (1960), Questors Theatre, London.
1961	Student productions of *Easy Death* at Oxford Playhouse, and the play for voices, *You've No Need to be Frightened*. Marriage to barrister David Harter.
1962	*The Ants*, first professional radio play, broadcast.
1963–9	Birth of three sons. Period of being at home with young children becomes politicizing experience. Churchill continues writing for radio: *Lovesick* (1966) and *Identical Twins* (1968) broadcast.
1971	Radio plays *Abortive* and *Not Not Not Not Not Enough Oxygen* broadcast.
1972	Radio plays *Schreber's Nervous Illness* and *Henry's Past* broadcast. Around time of *Schreber*, writes unperformed play *The Hospital at the Time of the Revolution*. *The Judge's Wife* broadcast on BBC television. First professional stage production, *Owners*, Royal Court Theatre Upstairs, London. *Schreber* given stage performance at King's Head Theatre, London.
1973	Radio play *Perfect Happiness* broadcast. *Owners* premièred in New York.
1974	*Turkish Delight* broadcast on BBC television. First

woman writer in residence at Royal Court Theatre.

1975   *Save it for the Minister*, with Mary O'Malley and Cherry Potter, broadcast on BBC television. Association with Royal Court continues with staging of *Objections to Sex and Violence* and *Moving Clocks Go Slow* (Theatre Upstairs). *Perfect Happiness* given a stage performance at Soho Poly, London.

1976   Begins working with companies: Joint Stock and Monstrous Regiment. *Light Shining in Buckinghamshire* performed at Traverse Theatre, Edinburgh; on tour, and at Royal Court Theatre Upstairs, London. Begins long association with director Max Stafford-Clark. *Vinegar Tom* performed at Humberside Theatre, Hull; on tour, and at ICA and Half Moon theatres, London.

1977   *Traps* performed at Royal Court Theatre Upstairs, London. Contributes to *Floorshow*, a touring cabaret, scripted with Bryony Lavery, Michelene Wandor and David Bradford.

1978   *The After-Dinner Joke* broadcast on BBC television. Writes unperformed play *Seagulls*.

1979   *The Legion Hall Bombing* broadcast on BBC television in censored version. Joint Stock production of *Cloud Nine* staged at Dartington College of Arts; on tour, and Royal Court Theatre, London.

1980   *Three More Sleepless Nights* staged at Soho Poly and Royal Court Theatre Upstairs, London.

1981   *Crimes* broadcast on television. *Cloud Nine* premièred in New York.

1982   *Top Girls*, staged at Royal Court Theatre, London, and subsequently transferred to New York. *Cloud Nine* wins Obie award.

1983   *Fen*, Joint Stock production, staged at University of Essex Theatre, Colchester; Almeida and Royal Court Theatres, London, and transferred to New York. *Top Girls* wins Obie award.

1984   *Softcops*, originally written in 1978, is given its first performance by the RSC at the Barbican Pit, London. Churchill contributes to a performance art production, *Midday Sun*, ICA, London, which marks her growing interest in non-text-based theatre. Winner of Susan

Smith Blackburn prize for *Fen*.

1985   First Methuen collection of plays published.

1986   *A Mouthful of Birds*, a Joint Stock production, co-written with David Lan, performed at Birmingham Repertory Theatre; on tour, and Royal Court Theatre, London. Production gives Churchill the opportunity of working with choreographer Ian Spink.

1987   *Serious Money* performed at Royal Court Theatre, London. Transfer to Wyndham's, London, and later to New York. Wins several theatre awards including a second Susan Smith Blackburn Award.

1988   Works again with Spink on *Fugue*, a dance-based piece, broadcast on Channel 4 television. *Serious Money* plays Broadway. *The Caryl Churchill Omnibus* broadcast on BBC television.

1989   *Icecream* staged at Royal Court Theatre, London. Churchill writes companion piece *Hot Fudge*, performed at Royal Court Theatre Upstairs, London.

1990   Churchill goes to Romania with drama students from Central School of Speech and Drama. Writes *Mad Forest*, 'a play from Romania', performed at Central and Royal Court Theatre, London, and National Theatre, Bucharest. Second Methuen collection of plays and *Churchill: Shorts* anthology published.

1991   *Lives of the Great Poisoners*, with Ian Spink and Orlando Gough, performed at Arnolfi, Bristol; on tour, and Riverside Studios, London. *Top Girls* broadcast on BBC television.

1994   *The Skriker* staged at the Cottesloe, Royal National Theatre, London. Translates *Thyestes*, staged at Royal Court Theatre Upstairs, London.

1997   *Hotel* performed by Second Stride at The Place Theatre, London, and *Blue Heart* premièred by Out of Joint. Third collection of plays published by Nick Hern.

Abbreviations

The two Methuen volumes of Churchill plays *Churchill: Plays One* and *Churchill: Plays Two* (London, 1985 and 1990) have been used throughout, cited in the text as *P*1 and *P*2 respectively, followed by the page number. The collection of short plays *Churchill: Shorts* (London: Hern, 1990) is abbreviated to *S*. Full details of the plays contained in these volumes can be found in the Select Bibliography.

Abbreviations for single plays are as follows:

H.	*Hotel*
IC	*Icecream*
LGP	*Lives of the Great Poisoners*
MB	*A Mouthful of Birds*
MF	*Mad Forest*
OSV	*Objections to Sex and Violence*
TS	*The Skriker*

Prologue

Caryl Churchill is widely acknowledged as a major contemporary British dramatist and leading figure on the international stage. While her theatre continues to receive popular critical attention and public acclaim, the woman behind the drama remains an intensely private person. In interviews (which she prefers not to give) Churchill, the writer, makes it clear that it is through her work that she wishes to be known.

This short study, therefore, gives an account of the writer through her work for the theatre and related media. Adopting a critically informed, introductory approach to key published and/or performed works, accessible to readers and spectators, the study begins with an overview of Churchill's early writing for radio, television and theatre, which has received less critical attention than some of her later stage plays. As testimony to the importance of Churchill's theatre in the context of contemporary women's drama and feminist theatre scholarship, Chapter 2 is devoted to an account of the emergent 'woman writer'. Chapter 3 examines the broader, socialist canvas of her playwriting, and the political perspective of her work also informs Chapter 4 which analyses the methodology and ideology of researching and dramatizing oppressed communities. The final chapter looks at Churchill's 'shapeshifting', innovative theatre-making which makes her plays radically resistant to classification or categorization.

What emerges is a Churchillian landscape which is characteristically 'frightening', greedy, corrupt, violent and damaged, and is populated with oppressed groups – particularly of women – marked by powerlessness, division and dispossession. In making visible the hidden realities of an unequal world, however, Churchill invites her spectators to share in the utopian possibility of an 'upside down world' – a veritable 'Cloud Nine'.

1

Beginnings: Radio, Stage and Television

> [I know] quite well what kind of society I would like: decentralized, nonauthoritarian, communist, nonsexist – a society in which people can be in touch with their feelings, and in control of their lives. But it always sounds both ridiculous and unattainable when you put it into words.[1]

Caryl Churchill has been performing her radical, revisionist view of society for over thirty years in professional theatre and is now acknowledged as one of the foremost, innovative writers for the contemporary stage.

She began to write as a young girl, producing mostly short stories and poems. When asked in interview whether she started to write 'because of a love of words' Churchill observed of herself:

> I don't know. That must be part of it. The fact that I was an only child may have helped. I had friends, but I did have quite a lot of time when I could be alone. Planning stories would be like solitary playing. I would invent a lot of characters, and descriptions of where they lived and maps, and it would be a whole game. So there was that sort of overlap. I also had a very close friend and we used to play a game which, looking back, reached a point where it was more like improvising plays.[2]

One recollection she offered with certainty, however, was her early interest in the theatre:

> I was also separately interested in the theatre. I liked going to plays. I used to want there to be plays done at school, and there weren't. When I was fifteen, I went off to a summer theatre in Canada, outside Montreal, and painted scenery. I didn't really put the two things together till a few years after that, at university.[3]

During her childhood in the 1940s, which was spent largely in London, and her teenage years in the 1950s, by which time the family had relocated to Montreal, Canada, Churchill recollects listening to the radio rather than watching television. Her writing as a young adult reflects the influence of this medium. Among her early works, for example, is the play for voices, *You've No Need to be Frightened* (1959), which was given a student production during Churchill's university years (1957–60), spent back in England at Lady Margaret Hall, Oxford. Her first professional production, *The Ants* (1962), although written with television in mind was, on the advice of her agent, Margaret Ramsay, put forward for radio broadcasting (P1 xi).

While linking her attraction to radio to the pleasure she derived from this medium in her formative years,[4] it is also significant that the solitary career of radio dramatist was one which Churchill was able to combine with her career as a mother of three sons, born between 1963 and 1969. In her own mother, Churchill had an example of a woman combining work with family life:

> She started out her life adventurously, leaving school at fourteen, working in an office, becoming a secretary and then a model ...There are wonderful photos of her saying, 'I'm so tired, but thanks to Ovaltine...' Later she began to get bit parts in films, and she went on with it after I was born, only stopping because of the war. I mostly remember my mother at home, but she did talk to me about working, and the fact that she used not to wear her wedding ring to work. I had the feeling, rather early on, that having a career was in no way incompatible with staying married and being very happy.[5]

Later, the issue of women, families and work would be debated and taken up by Churchill in the politics of major plays such as *Top Girls* and *Fen*.

Meanwhile, Churchill also began to write for stage and television. In her father, a cartoonist by profession, she had contact with someone who was working in images, although it was only later, she confesses, that she began to make connections between their respective crafts: 'Cartoons are really so much like plays. An image with somebody saying something'.[6] She recollects writing about 'ten other plays' for theatre and television during the 1960s and early 1970s (P1 xi).[7]

4

Although she continued to write for television until 1981 when *Crimes* was broadcast, and returned briefly to the medium in 1988 for her dance-drama collaboration *Fugue*, the 1970s might be seen as a phasing out of her interest in television work. On the other hand, writing for the stage was to become increasingly important during this decade of her artistic career.

Churchill's early work reflects a number of the stylistic and thematic concerns of her later stage plays. Experimenting with traditional approaches to dramatic writing, playing with the conventions of form, time, narrative, structure, language and dialogue are stylistically evident in the early dramas. In the radio plays, the power structures of marital and familial relations are thematized in *The Ants* (1962), *Lovesick* (1966), *Abortive* (1971), *Henry's Past* (1972) and *Perfect Happiness* (1973); identity in crisis is presented in *Identical Twins* (1968) and the schizophrenic world of *Schreber's Nervous Illness* (1972), and 'madness... sweeping the country' in a world starved of natural resources is depicted in *Not Not Not Not Not Enough Oxygen* (1971). The unperformed stage play *The Hospital at the Time of the Revolution*, written at the same time as *Schreber's Nervous Illness*, again looks at madness, but in the specific context of colonial war, and Churchill's early play for television *The Judge's Wife* (1972) questions reactionary politics with revolutionary action.

Rather than survey all of this early work, this chapter will focus on a cross-section of writing for radio, stage and television. The selection is designed to illustrate Churchill's early preoccupation with 'madness and civilization', and explores her critique of the regulating systems of authority which determine 'normal' behaviour, and, conversely, marginalize and police the 'abnormal', sexually 'deviant', 'insane' or 'criminal', and so on. Although this work dates from the mid-1960s to the early 1970s, the gender politics (and racial politics in *The Hospital*) stage a number of issues pertinent to current feminist theorizings of sexuality, power, subjectivity, cultural identity and the (de-)construction of gender.

'LOVE'S CURE': *LOVESICK*

Lovesick, Churchill's second professionally broadcast radio play (1966), focuses on the attempts of a psychiatrist, Dr Hodge, to 'cure' or 'correct' the 'deviant' desires of his patients and friends through aversion therapy. Aversion therapy was a form of medical treatment in which patients were administered nausea-inducing drugs and were confronted with images of their 'abnormal' desires. In theory, a patient would be 'cured' of his or her 'lovesickness' as he or she learnt to associate a 'deviant' desire with the nausea and vomiting. In the radio play, for example, Hodge describes how he successfully 'cured' a 'dowdy nymphomaniac':

> First she was given a drug which causes nausea and then photographs of naked men. I wasn't sure if photographs would be enough so at a later stage I put my extraordinarily unquestioning and really stupid assistant Jenks into her room and told him to undress. To my delight she vomited repeatedly. (S 10–11)

In the 1950s, aversion therapy was especially used to 'cure' homosexual patients of their 'perverse' desires, a practice which Churchill critiques in the radio play when a homosexual 'cure' goes wrong and ends in suicide.

The narrative thread of *Lovesick* involves a complex weaving of 'illicit' relationships. Through Jessica Zolotov, who is having an affair with Hodge's friend Max, married to Lucy, Hodge is introduced to Ellen McNab. While working on a 'cure' for Ellen's alcoholic aunt, he becomes obsessed with Ellen. Although married, Ellen desires Kevin, one of Jessica's two sons, while Kevin is interested in starting a homosexual relationship. Like a modern Racinian tragedy, the chain of unrequited desires is further complicated by Jessica's feigned interest in Max as a means of countering her incestuous relationship with her other son, Robert. Ultimately, Hodge attempts to 'cure' Kevin of his homosexuality, and to treat Ellen's desire for Kevin and her phobia of him. His designs are thwarted by Robert, who intervenes and deceives Hodge's assistant into reversing instructions so that Ellen has Kevin's cure, is disgusted by men and falls in love with her female nurse, and Kevin, with Ellen's cure, hates himself but is desperately in love with Hodge.

Hodge functions as the key narrative voice. The act of narration reverses his empowered position as psychiatrist and places him in the disempowered role of patient. As confessor, story-teller, it is Hodge who is in the psychiatrist's chair, and the

radio audience who is positioned as 'doctor' hearing the
confessed narrative. This technique of role reversal is central
to Churchill's critique of the policing of desire. It calls into
question the criteria of sexual behaviour by which the white,
middle-class, male psychiatrist – now positioned as patient –
judges 'normalcy'. Hodge's 'cure' of the rapist and murderer,
for example, 'privately' told to the listening audience, or doctor,
takes on the tone of a 'criminal' confession:

> Another remarkable cure was Smith, the rapist and murderer. The
> papers were full of his mutilated victims but to my joy he came to
> me before the police knew anything about him. Max wanted me to
> castrate him but my usual method was perfectly successful, leaving
> only a slight distaste for sex and butchers in an otherwise well-
> balanced personality. He is back at work, the joy, as always, of his old
> parents, and my only worry is that the police may yet catch him and
> hold him responsible for his corpses. (S 11)

Moreover, Hodge's attempt to 'cure' Kevin of his homosexuality
and Kevin's subsequent suicide highlight the dangers of
regulating sexuality. Hodge's own heterosexual position is
further undermined as he confesses to a suppression of
homosexual desire:

> I [Hodge] might have persuaded him [Kevin] to have treatment, he
> loved me enough to do anything for me. More than anyone else has
> ever done. But I was too disheartened to start again at once and he
> killed himself before I got down to it...I've homosexual tendencies
> like anyone else, but well suppressed, and it was most inconvenient
> to have them stirred. (S 18)

Ultimately, the characters liberate themselves into sexually
'transgressive' positions: Ellen finds a lesbian relationship with
her nurse; Jessica remains in a relationship with her son Robert;
and Max returns to his wife, Lucy, in a role-reversal relationship
where Lucy goes out to work in 'trouser suits' and Max stays at
home and feels comfortable in 'wearing her [Lucy's] pink silk
dress and blue toque' (S 17). Conversely, it is Hodge who is left
in need of treatment. As the play ends, he prepares, hesitantly,
to apply aversive therapy to his own heterosexual ('normal')
desires for Ellen:

> I have a photograph of Ellen on my desk. I've plenty more, and I will
> take the drug in just a minute. It can't be fear of nausea that makes

me hesitate. By next week, if I don't turn back, I could be free to concentrate on my work, with no thought of Ellen, whose beauty is great. (S 19)

The isolation of the heterosexual male in a group of repressed sexual 'deviants', whose forbidden desires surface through aversion to prescriptive heterosexual role play, is a model which Churchill would later use in the writing of Cloud Nine.

'THE FEMALE MALADY': *SCHREBER'S NERVOUS ILLNESS*

In contrast to *Lovesick*, *Schreber's Nervous Illness*, broadcast on radio in 1972, presents the narrative viewpoint of the schizophrenic patient, Daniel Paul Schreber. Schreber was the subject of one of Freud's case studies, written shortly before Schreber's death in 1911.[8] Churchill's source material was Schreber's memoirs, first published in 1903, and translated in 1955 as *Memoirs of My Nervous Illness* (S 58).

Schreber is set in asylums in Leipzig and Dresden around the turn of the century. The voice of Schreber's psychiatrist, Dr Weber, punctuates Schreber's narrative of madness with clinical diagnoses, descriptions of the patient's behaviour, symptoms, and so on. Significant in Schreber's narrative is the descent into madness of a man who was a high-status, authority figure; a former president of the Court of Appeal in Dresden. However, he works through the paranoid delusions of his first breakdown in which he saw his doctor, Professor Flechsig, as persecutor, as 'soul murderer', and comes to terms with the divine sufferings he believes he experiences through his body, which he hears as voices or 'rays', in a bid to be discharged from the asylum. Ironically, it is to the Appeal Court of which he was once the president that he has to make his application for freedom, which is finally granted. Schreber's comment on his starting life outside of the asylum again challenges the definition of what is judged to be 'sane' or 'mad'. Describing his need to control his 'bellowing' in public, one of the remaining symptoms of his illness, Schreber concludes:

> While going for walks along country roads or in fields I make things easy for myself and simply let the bellowing happen. Sometimes it continues for five or ten minutes, during which time I feel perfectly

well. Anyone who saw me would, however, hardly understand what I was doing, and might really think he was seeing a madman. (S 93)

That Weber makes brief comments on or offers explanations for Schreber's condition, but is not heard conversing or communicating with Schreber directly, is significant in the context of the radio play's social and cultural production. The 1960s witnessed a rebellion against traditional methods of psychiatry: a rejection of shock treatments, ECT, the isolated institutionalization of patients, and so on. The publication of R. D. Laing's influential study of *The Divided Self* (1960) was, for a time, a controversial but seminal reference point calling for a different approach to psychiatric care – one based on close communication between patient and doctor; on dialogue rather than clinical diagnosis. Laing's work influenced a number of writers, among them playwrights David Mercer, who wrote the television play *In Two Minds* (1967), which was later made into a film, and David Edgar, who used the contemporary case study of one of Laing's patients for his stage play *Mary Barnes* (1977). Churchill's radio play may, therefore, be seen as part of the contemporary debate on schizophrenia. Her play, however, differs from the other two examples in so far as it uses the turn-of-the-century memoirs to treat a contemporary issue in dramatic form, rather than making use of modern case studies. Interrogating the present through staging a (historical) past is a strategy central to several of Churchill's subsequent stage plays.

Looking at *Schreber* through a modern feminist framework of approaches to psychiatry and psychoanalysis makes the 'unmanning' of Schreber's body – his description of a resistance to, but gradual acceptance of a process of feminization – of particular interest. In the field of French feminist theory and psychoanalytic writing, for example, Hélène Cixous's *l'écriture féminine* examines the binary opposition of Woman as Other than man, and calls for women to struggle against 'conventional man' in order to write themselves into being.[9] In her radio play, Churchill uses the body of the 'conventional man' to 'write', or rather to stage, the feminine Other. Critic Amelia Howe Kritzer develops this point by applying Elaine Showalter's concept of 'the female malady' – based on the binary opposition between rationality/masculinity and madness/femininity – to her analysis of *Schreber*.[10] Kritzer explains:

9

Churchill uses as her main character a man afflicted with the 'female malady' of madness, rather than a woman reacting madly to the world of male-imposed structures. In taking an approach that defies habitual divisions and avoids reinforcing such division, Churchill emphasizes that any individual – male or female – may be both a perpetrator and a victim of patriarchal oppression. At the same time, Schreber's story, as presented in this radio play, gives a compelling capsulization of the relation of women to patriarchal power.[11]

Hence, like Hodge, who is doctor and patient, Schreber the erstwhile judge and patriarch encodes masculinity and power; Schreber the patient embodies femininity and disempowerment.

Schreber's contact with the feminine Other is experienced not through logos (speech), which he uses in his madness to rationalize an exclusion of the feminine, but through the body as he imagines his physical transformation from man to woman:

> I am preoccupied with changing into a woman...Now the voluptuousness was so great that some rays began to like entering my body. I considered it my right and duty to cultivate feelings of voluptuousness. Few people have been brought up according to such strict moral principles as I or practised such moderation in matters of sex. But to attract the rays I must image myself as man and woman in one person having intercourse with myself. (S 78)

The possibility of moving beyond the gender divide lies in the androgynous play of Schreber's madness. It is significant, however, that the possibility of 'voluptuousness', or the potential for what Cixous might call in her writing *jouissance* (total joy or ecstasy), can only be expressed in the space of the asylum. In the real, 'sane' world, into which 'conventional man' is returned, the binary order of masculine versus feminine is not to be transgressed. When, like Max in *Lovesickness*, Schreber takes pleasure in dressing his body in signs of conventional femininity, and describes 'standing in front of the mirror with ribbons and cheap necklaces on my body', he admits that this is 'the only thing that could be considered unreasonable' by the ('sane') world outside the asylum (S 88). Repression of the feminine is necessary for Schreber to secure his release. As he 'rationalizes' in his state of madness, 'nothing can exist permanently which is against the Order of the World' (S 80–1). The dis-orderly world of theatre can, however, make visible utopian possibilities of gender play, as Churchill would further show in the cross-dressing strategies of

Cloud Nine or the androgynous playing in *A Mouthful of Birds.*

'BLACK SKINS, WHITE MASKS': *THE HOSPITAL AT THE TIME OF THE REVOLUTION*

Written at the time of *Schreber*, *The Hospital* is an unstaged play which also examines madness. The action is set in 1956 in the Blida-Joinville Hospital in Algeria during the Algerian war. The central protagonist is Frantz Fanon who was head of the psychiatric unit at Blida-Joinville, a position he later resigned from to join in the War of National Liberation fought by the Algerian people. Fanon's writing on the links between mental disorders and colonial war was a key source for the *Hospital*, and details extracted from his case studies are woven into Churchill's dramatization.[12]

For example, Churchill's three Algerian patients, referred to as A, B, and C, are drawn from Fanon's series of patient case studies which detail different psychotic reactions and disorders as a result of war, specifically colonial war. Patient A suffers from the delayed shock of having been responsible for killing a number of people in the bombing of a bar. B is a torture victim who tries to hang himself in the hospital when he sees his torturer – a European police inspector who has been admitted as a patient to the hospital, but whom B, in his state of trauma, believes has come to torture him again. Patient C is a light-skinned Algerian who is paranoid that everyone mistakes him for a European and believes him to be a coward and traitor of his Algerian people:

> I've never been interested in politics, only in engineering, and there's nothing wrong with that. You wouldn't say I was a European would you? I've a pale skin but that's from being ill and indoors so much. You wouldn't say I was a European? To look at me you'd see I was an Algerian, wouldn't you, just by looking at me. (*S* 120)

The colonial issue of 'Black Skins, White Masks'[13] is not only a thematic concern in *The Hospital*, but race also informs Churchill's techniques of theatricalization. For the staging and costuming she instructs that the 'black skins' of the Algerians be set in the 'bare white walls' of the hospital (*S* 97). Medicine, the

11

hospital, is associated with Western 'civilization'; the 'sick' Algerians are there to be 'cured', colonized by the West. Fanon, as a Black doctor from Martinique who trained in Paris, signs the schizophrenic split of colonizer and colonized on and through the white (European) uniform of medicine on his Black skin. As a doctor, he has to treat both the white colonizers, stressed and traumatized by the acts of torture they carry out, and their Black victims.

In addition to the writings of Fanon, Churchill also acknowledges a debt to R. D. Laing as a source for *The Hospital* (*S* 96). Churchill's interest in Laing can be most obviously traced in the dramatization of Françoise, daughter of the '*middle-aged Europeans*' Monsieur and Madame (*S* 97). Françoise is brought by her parents to Fanon for treatment of a behavioural disorder which Fanon subsequently diagnoses as schizophrenia. Françoise's illness is identified by her parents as the progressive degeneration of a 'good' daughter who turns 'bad'; whose actions become so increasingly abnormal that she has to be 'mad'. This is a pattern which Laing discusses in his case study of Julie and which he attributes in part to the infantilization of the child which hinders the autonomy, or sense of self, in the adolescent adult.[14] Françoise is similarly infantilized by her parents, particularly her mother, and Churchill writes this on to her body in the direction '*she is neatly and prettily dressed in a style rather too young*' (*S* 97).

However, Françoise's case is further complicated by the colonial war. Her father, the colonizer, tortures his victims in their home and Françoise hears their screams in the night: 'My mother has killed a little girl. But no one punishes her, do they? My father has killed far more people. I can't give you a list of the names but I hear the screams all night' (*S* 113–14). The 'sick' or 'murdered' daughter of the colonial oppressors mirrors the position of the colonized – a loss of self, identity, culture and race due to the violent imposition of white, Western values. Infantilization and colonialization are explicitly linked as the parents attempt to police the 'bad' child by keeping her locked up, just like the 'natives' who are brought in for questioning. The starved body Françoise believes to be poisoned by her mother, and which she sees as already dead, is also a body poisoned and murdered by the colonial war. Starving the body expresses her guilt as a 'sick' daughter of the West.[15] The final scene is of Fanon and Françoise, sitting first in silence, and then Françoise trying to explain her absent body to Fanon:

> Under the dress I can't find where I am. So when I take it off there's nobody there. They can't see Françoise because she was taken off upstairs and nobody came downstairs and into the room. My mother made that dress to kill me. It ate me away. That was a poison dress I put on. (*S* 146)

The 'frightening' future for the disempowered daughter in the patriarchal, capitalist, colonizing systems of the West, is an issue which Churchill raises in later plays – most obviously represented in the figure of Angie in *Top Girls*.

CRIME AND PUNISHMENT: *THE JUDGE'S WIFE*

The Judge's Wife, Churchill's first drama to be broadcast on television (1972), reflects a shift from the psychiatric and psychoanalytic questions of 'madness and civilization' in medicine, to the political and existential questions of autonomy, law, order and 'civilized' behaviour in the legal system. The Judge, who is designated by title and role, rather than represented as an individual, named person, is the 'conventional man' of authority Schreber presumably once was. Crime and punishment are problematized in the play, which opens with the shooting of the Judge by Michael Warren, brother of a revolutionary 'criminal' Vernon Warren, whom the Judge has sentenced to a heavy prison term. Who is the criminal? Is the Judge's sentencing of Vernon Warren 'criminal'? Are the nonspecified violent revolutionary acts of Vernon Warren criminal or just? Is the shooting of the Judge a crime or suitable punishment for the act of sentencing? The shooting of the Judge is played and re-played in the drama, while events leading up to the shooting are dramatized through domestic scenes in the Judge's household between the Judge, his wife Caroline, her sister Barbara, and the maid, Peg.

As in *The Hospital*, power is encoded in vestimentary signs of authority: the white coat of the doctor, the robes of the judge. When these are removed, as, for example, in a domestic scene when the Judge is seen preparing for a bath with the help of his subservient wife, then the reality of the powerless '*naked, fat, old, defenceless, body*' is exposed (S 150). Identity is therefore at risk when people fail to recognize, or reject and rebel against the authority signed on the public body. As the Judge explains to his wife with regard to Warren, 'I was trying my right to exist' (S 156). It is only by playing out the role of judiciary to an extreme that the Judge feels able to exist. As in Jean Genet's theatre, in plays such as *The Blacks* or *The Maids*, if you represent authority you play authority until it is played out. If you are cast in the role of the enemy, then you have the freedom to play the enemy to a violent extreme, until the role is unmasked. The repeated, ritualized death of the Judge is a playing out, critique and destruction of the authority which constitutes his identity. In a monologue delivered in the presence of her sister Barbara after the 'death' of her husband, Caroline rationalizes his death as follows:

> He had become the enemy. He loathed himself. He said he would commit suicide. And then at a brilliant stroke he saw what he could do for other people. He could be the enemy... He could live out his way of life but more extremely... He could use his power unjustly so that someone would be forced to take it away from him. (S 162)

When she speaks, however, she speaks, as the title of the play indicates, as the Judge's wife. In the private, domestic sphere, she is seen in her role as the subservient wife. At a mirror in the bedroom, she is shown trying out a smiling mask. Its artificiality is exposed as she tries on the smile and lets it slip. Only after the 'death' of her husband does she move beyond the public gaze of the mirror when she appears alongside her sister in a '*dressing-gown*', with '*her hair... unbrushed, her face crumpled*' (S 161). Now her sister is her mirror: '*they are two old women*' (S 161). In narrating and rationalizing her husband's death she finally plays out her own role as the Judge's wife. The disempowerment of the women characters, especially the Irish maid who rebels against her imperialist, English 'master' by leaving her employment, raises gender oppression as an issue in the use and abuse of power.

The crime and punishment narrative in *The Judge's Wife* is dramatized in a non-naturalistic style. The repeated flashbacks of the shooting disrupt narrative linearity and chronology.

Identity is unfixed in the doubling of roles as one actor plays both Michael and Vernon Warren, a device which poses the question – who really kills the Judge? Scenes from outside the courtroom, a public sphere, are meta-theatrically represented on a television screen in the Judge's bedroom, a private space, and so on. In short, this early television play is replete with techniques of destabilization which are precursors of theatrical devices Churchill subsequently develops in her theatre. Although Patrick Campbell, reviewing for *Stage and Television Today* was critical of the play for being 'one of those plays which leave the critic with a strong sense of frustration, seeing so much originality just failing in the event to fulfil its promise',[17] it is the 'promise' of things to come which, retrospectively, strikes the reader and viewer. From this point of view, *The Judge's Wife* illustrates Churchill's early preoccupation with finding innovative forms to work in (a point taken up and pursued in Chapter 5 of this study). As Churchill herself explains:

> I do enjoy the form of things. I enjoy finding the form that seems best to fit what I'm thinking about. I don't set out to find a bizarre way of writing. I certainly don't think that you have to force it. But, on the whole, I enjoy plays that are non naturalistic and don't move at real time.[18]

As a selection of Churchill's early writings was not widely available until the publication of the anthology *Shorts* in 1990, the 'beginnings' of her writing career have not, as yet, received all the critical interest due to them from women's studies. While, for example, Cixous's stage play *Portrait of Dora* (1979), which restages Freud's case study of Dora and undermines the traditional power relations between the empowered psychiatrist and disempowered female patient, has received much feminist critical attention, Churchill's en-gendered explorations of 'madness and civilization', as discussed here, have not.

Elsewhere I have argued that women's studies may find a valuable source of critical practice in the form of feminist theatre: a medium which makes visible its theoretical and critical concerns on and through the body.[19] I would want to argue that Churchill's staging of the body in her early work, whether this is the 'cured', 'unmanned', 'feminine' or 'colonized' body of the oppressed, or the representation of conventional man' as oppressor, has much to offer current thinking in the fields of feminist, queer and post-colonial theory.

However, while recognition is still due to the early work from feminist and gender thinking in other forms, the plays presented and examined in the next chapter show how the emergent concerns of Churchill as the 'woman writer' have been instrumental in shaping and defining the theory, criticism and practice of feminist theatre studies.

2

The 'Woman Writer'

In 1977 Ann McFerran conducted an interview for *Time Out* with nine British women playwrights, and headed the commentaries with the statement 'the male-dominated theatre is giving way (somewhat)'.[1] In retrospect, our 'male-dominated theatre' hardly seems to have given way at all, but those women in touch with the Second Women's Liberation Movement in the 1970s were, in the climate of feminism, able to view the possibility of a more equitable future with a degree of optimism. Gillian Hanna, a founding company member of Monstrous Regiment, with whom Churchill worked on *Vinegar Tom* (1976) and the *Floorshow* cabaret (1977), recollects:

> Feminism was leaping in our heads...To be a woman in 1975 and not to have felt the excitement of things starting to change, possibilities in the air, would have meant that you were only half alive...
>
> ...we wanted to change the world. At the time, this didn't seem like such an outrageous project. All around us, women in every area of the world we knew were doing the same thing. It seemed as natural as breathing.
>
> But much more exciting than breathing. Exhilarating. The sense of being in the right place at the right time, in step with a great movement in history, *part* of history, making history ourselves. We were part of a huge wave of women and we were going to remake everything. It gradually dawned on us that we didn't have to go out and join any movement. We were already in it. We were the Movement.[2]

If change was not immediate, then feminism at least enabled women to express their discontents, or, as Churchill argued in McFerran's interview, 'one of the things the Women's Movement has done is to show the way the traps work'.[3] The 'traps'

17

specific to theatre, which the women playwrights discussed in McFerran's interview, included male bias of their profession, the paucity of roles for women, the ways in which their voices had not been heard in the theatre, and the difficulties of combining a playwriting career with motherhood.

When questioned about her writing and feminism, Churchill observed:

> For years and years I thought of myself as a writer before I thought of myself as a woman, but recently I've found that I would say I was a feminist writer as opposed to other people saying I was. I've found that as I go out more into the world and get into situations which involve women what I feel is quite strongly a feminist position and that inevitably comes into what I write.[4]

Churchill went on to state that in her early writing she replicated the dominant tradition of the male writer by making her central characters with 'some knotty problem male', because as a 'woman writer' she felt she had to show that she too 'could do it'. Subsequently, however, 'realising the bad deal women have had' she made the 'characters with the knotty problems women'.[5] It was not just a question of concentrating on female rather than male characters, but of thinking through 'the "maleness" of the traditional structure of plays, with conflict and building in a certain way to a climax'.[6]

Among Churchill's work in the early 1970s, for example, are two unpublished plays which show her challenging the 'maleness' of writing and experimenting with an all-female and emergent feminist aesthetic: the radio play *Perfect Happiness* (1973) and the television play *Turkish Delight* (1974).[7] *Perfect Happiness* raises class and gender issues as two female office employees have an encounter with the middle-class wife of their employer. Set in a middle-class kitchen, it offers a critique of bourgeois domesticity enacted through women. The absent presence of the husband and employer figure, heard arriving at the end of the play after the working-class women have alleged they murdered him, is a technique also used in *Turkish Delight*, where the female characters are objectified and defined by their relationship to an unseen male figure, John. Set at a masquerade party where the women are in harem costuming, the aesthetic and ideological work of the play explores the kinds of issues which would preoccupy feminist film, and, subsequently, theatre studies in the 1980s: the gaze, objectification of women, the masquerade of femininity, and women as objects of exchange within a masculine, phallocentric economy'.[8] Whereas in the 1970s Churchill's feminist subjects and experimental forms both excited and baffled theatre critics (see for example the discussion of *Vinegar Tom*'s reception), in the 1980s, her critiques of gender – most especially those in *Cloud Nine* and *Top Girls* – helped to shape and to define the growing body of feminist writing, in theory, criticism and practice, which constitutes the field now recognized as feminist theatre studies.

In order to look at the emergent and evolving feminism of Churchill, the 'woman writer', I propose in this chapter to sample full-length stage plays from a ten-year period of playwriting: from the formative, gender-inflected critique of *Owners* (1972), to the mature, materialist-feminist inquiry of *Top Girls* (1982).

MASCULINE ECONOMY/FEMININE 'OTHER': *OWNERS*

Performed at the Royal Court Theatre Upstairs in 1972, Churchill's first full-length stage play is a critical analysis of Western capitalism's preoccupation with ownership. In staging her critique she brought together two working ideas: 'there was one idea going on about landlords and tenants, and then another about western aggressiveness and eastern passivity, and I realised that obviously the two could go together'.[9] Churchill dramatizes the 'haves and have nots' of the property market in her representation of the property-owning childless couple, Marion and Clegg, and the tenants, Alec and Lisa, who, in reduced circumstances, share rooms in a house with their two boys and Alec's mother. Lisa has a third child on the way as the play begins. 'Western aggressiveness and eastern passivity' are marked in the characters of Marion and Alec respectively. Churchill explains that gender role-reversal helped to make the contrast clear: 'the landlord became a woman, because that made the distinction better than if I'd had an active man and a passive woman'.[10]

As an ex-psychiatric patient who refused feminine condition-ing as part of her treatment, Marion, on exiting from hospital, elected to enter the financial world of property owning:

> CLEGG: When Marion was in hospital they tried to tell her she'd be happier and more sane as a good wife. Comb your hair and take an interest in your husband's work...But she wouldn't listen. She came out of there with staring eyes and three weeks later she bought her first house.
>
> (P1 10)

Like Marlene in *Top Girls*, Marion demonstrates that the capitalist impulse is not determined by the biological difference between male and female, but illustrates how women may also take on the values of the masculine. That Marion is driven by the desire to own and to control, but is not fully in control of her own actions, is signified in the directions for her costuming: *'her clothes are expensive but often badly matched, coming undone, slightly askew'* (P1 5).

The desire to own, to appropriate, is also shared by Marion's husband, Clegg. In the opening to the play Clegg is seen in his butcher's shop which is about to go out of business. However, Clegg explains that because he has no son to leave the business to there is no need for him to keep a business going:

> I envisaged a chain. Clegg and Son. I was still the son at the time. I would have liked a son myself once I was the Clegg. But now I've no business I don't need a son. Having no son I don't need a business'.
> (P1 9)

Clegg's rationale of his business and lack of a son and heir reflect the values, needs and ethos of capitalist and patriarchal systems.

By contrast, Alec and Lisa represent the dispossessed group: the tenants and victims of the owning classes. Passive resistance to Marion's active attempts to turn them out of their rented rooms is encoded in the figure of Alec. As Churchill observes, the dynamic between Alec and Marion is an embodiment of East and West values. Although Alec may be momentarily (sexually) engaged with Marion, he cannot be owned. He does not 'keep' (P1 32). Driven by her impulse to possess him, Marion declares her desire for Alec in terms of ownership, representing herself in imperialist and masculinist discourse:

I'm yours whether you want me or not. Have all the money and stay here too if that's what you want. Empires have been lost for love. Worlds well lost. We men of destiny get what we're after even if we're destroyed by it. And everyone else with us. We split the atom. Onward. Love me. (P 31)

Similarly, Clegg represents his relationship with Marion as a financial one; as a commodity for investment, profit and loss: 'I have invested heavily in Marion and don't intend to lose any part of my profit' (P1 56).

Alec, on the other hand, occupies a position which has no investment in a materialist economy. Having, as he explains to Marion, been troubled by the difficulty of not seeing the point of anything in life, including taking his own life (P1 47), Alec was able to transcend this position to a state of selfless passivity. When he takes the life of his mother by disconnecting her drip in hospital, the act is not an investment in an economy of the self, but a selfless act in the interests of the other. Similarly, when, in the conclusion of the play, he goes back into their burning home to save a baby, it is not his 'own' baby which he saves, but the baby from another family.

A central figure in Churchill's critique of ownership is Worsely, Marion's go-between who, acting on her behalf, tries to get tenants out of the properties Marion is buying. Clegg draws Worsely into his schemes to kill Marion – to possess her in the only way he can – and, at various times, Clegg and Marion enlist Worsely's help to fatally harm Alec – Clegg because he does not wish to lose Marion to Alec, and Marion because she cannot succeed in owning Alec. Much of the dark comedy in *Owners* is driven by Worsely's Ortonesque, farcical attempts to commit suicide. Worsely believes that he owns what he stands up in, his 'flesh and blood', in contrast to the Samaritan he describes as having befriended him, whom Worsely reports as arguing that God is 'the almighty landlord', and 'life is leasehold' (P1 35). Each time Worsely makes an appearance in the play, his body is marked by further self-inflicted damage, but he never quite succeeds in 'owning', that is, deciding the destiny of his own body.

Worsely is pivotal to Churchill's sinister style of comedy which arises out of the juxtaposition of light and dark tones. As drama scholar Martin Esslin, reviewing the production,

21

described, 'what is remarkable is that this play which has such deep undertones is on the surface a highly amusing folk-comedy'.[11] Moreover as Esslin further observed, the juxtaposition of stylistic registers was also encoded in the original stage design for *Owners* which represented 'the hospital and the butcher's shop in their full naturalistic reality in front of a stylised back cloth'.[12]

Writing at the time of the production, Churchill identified Lisa as the 'victim of the story', and commented on how she had originally conceived the character in traditional terms as the woman who owns in a conventional way – 'my house, my husband, my children, my family'.[13] It is precisely her position as a woman within the traditional setting of home, husband, children and family, which makes her a victim. Reading *Owners* through Hélène Cixous's psychoanalytic framing of gender (as introduced in the discussion of *Schreber*), then Lisa is the Other which has to be colonized in the interests of the masculine 'selfsame'[14] (as is Alec when he refuses to be possessed by Marion). As the feminine Other, Lisa is the object of 'reappropriation'; she has to be owned, victimized, in order to confirm 'male privilege'; to repress the threat of castration.[15] This is clearly represented when in trying to get her baby back she allows Clegg to 'fuck' her. When Clegg reneges on his promise to help, she verbally assaults his masculinity: 'look at you sweating like a bit of hot fat, which is what you are. With your belly sagging like a black pudding and your poor little pork sausage' (*P1* 54). The meat imagery disavows rather than confirms the mastery of Clegg the butcher, or, read metaphorically, the butchery of the masculine, phallocentric order.

The victimization of Lisa is further, and perhaps most significantly, established in the loss of her baby to Marion and Clegg. Lisa's labour coincides with her discovery of the possibility of an affair between Marion and Alec being resumed. In her distress, and in labour, she refuses to bring the baby back to their home, saying she'd rather kill it, and then she challenges Marion to look after it. After the birth, and in a state of distress, she is coerced by Marion and Worsely into signing papers, and 'legally' makes over her baby to Marion and Clegg:

LISA: . . . I can't read it.
MARION: No need.

WORSELY: Sign here.
LISA: After can I see the baby?
WORSELY: Don't drip all over the paper.
LISA: I want to see he's all right.
MARION: Of course he is.
LISA. Because later when I'm better I'll have him back.
WORSELY: He's very well taken care of. I wouldn't lie.
Lisa signs the paper.

(*P1* 42–3)

Churchill's dialogue heightens Lisa's disempowered position. She is no match for Worsely and Marion. She cannot even see the papers she is signing because of her tears. As psychologist and psychotherapist Phyllis Chesler, writing on surrogacy, adoption and custody issues, comments:

> What else is it but 'duress' to obtain a birth mother's signature by offering her hospital care or money when she's about to go into labor or has literally just given birth: when she's experiencing the most stressful moment of her life; when she has no legal advice, no job or housing or prospects...Most adoption papers are signed under 'duress' and most should therefore be considered illegal.[16]

What, in Lisa's case, begins as a form of protest – I'd rather kill or surrender my baby than accept the victim-position – rebounds under 'duress', as the birth mother signs away the rights to her baby. As actual surrogacy cases in the 1980s (the most (in)famous of these being the Baby M case in America)[17] have shown. 'owning' or buying babies is a class and gender issue: economic privilege empowers one class of mothers and fathers to buy: economic deprivation encourages disempowered mothers to sell. Lisa, as Churchill's dramatic representation of the economically deprived birth mother is, therefore, as much a victim of her class as of her gender.

As the birth father, Alec also critiques the politics of fatherhood which insist on the need for a son and heir. Alec does not seek to 'own' the baby as the natural father, and he cares for, indeed, as already noted, dies for a child which is not his 'own'. Unlike Clegg, who wants to keep the baby to fulfil his patriarchal desire for a son to inherit his business, or Marion, who wants the baby as her way of owning a part of Alec (*P1* 62), Alec does not assert his own claims to the child.

Legislative and social concern for the rights of the father has become a (frightening) issue for mothers in the 1990s.[18] Although this would inflect a revival of *Owners* differently to the play's 1970s social and cultural context, when motherhood figured on the middle-class feminist agenda as a contested site of maternal destiny,'[19] it would also invest the play with renewed topicality for the 1990s. Similarly, it is difficult to read another of Churchill's early radio plays, *Not Not Not Not Not Enough Oxygen*, broadcast in 1971, the year before *Owners*, where, in a world running out of natural resources, the birthing of children has to be sanctioned by a paid for licence, without thinking of the recently broadcast pictures of the dying rooms in China.[20] Churchill herself comments that 'it's slightly unnerving to read *Not...Oxygen* twenty years later. It's more obviously relevant now than it was then' (*S* intro).[21] Or, as poet and playwright Jackie Kay, interviewing Churchill in the late 1980s, put it to her, 'you seem to be able to predict popular concerns before they become popular'.[22]

Finally, it is also important to note in the context of the motherhood issue, that this was also one of immediate, personal concern to Churchill. She has described how her preliminary ideas for *Owners* were interrupted by a miscarriage, and how the writing of the play took place immediately, and rather hurriedly, in a few painful days, less than a week after coming out of hospital:

> I wrote it in three days. I'd just come out of hospital after a particularly gruesome late miscarriage. Still quite groggy and my arm ached because they'd given me an injection that didn't work. Into it went for the first time a lot of things that had been building up in me over a long time, political attitudes as well as personal ones.[23]

It is precisely this personal experience which increasingly politicized Churchill in moving from thinking of herself as a 'writer before I thought of myself as a woman', to thinking of herself as a 'feminist writer'.[24]

THE 'OFFSIDE BODY': *VINEGAR TOM*

Working within collaborative structures, with writers, companies, directors, and so on, also provided a way for the personal to become increasingly political and feminist in Churchill's career as a dramatist. For example, two of the other women playwrights involved in McFerran's 1977 interview, Mary O'Malley and Cherry Potter, worked with Churchill in the mid-1970s on a television piece, *Save It for the Minister*, which looked at sex discrimination. More significant, however, was her 1976 production of *Vinegar Tom* with Monstrous Regiment, and *Light Shining in Buckinghamshire*, written at the same time for Joint Stock (see chapter 3).

Up until this point, Churchill's writing career had been, as she described it, a 'solitary' one (P1 129) Chris Bowler of Monstrous Regiment recollected talking to Churchill about her more solitary career, as compared, for example, with life in the company:

> the difference ... is that she was involved in child care over a number of years and started writing for the radio at home. As a result she was always at one remove. I remember talking to her years ago when she said that that was what it felt like, being at one remove. She felt that being at home she had missed out on things that we were involved in.[25]

In consequence, Churchill was both excited and daunted by the prospect of being able to work on a feminist piece with and for a feminist company: 'I felt briefly shy and daunted, wondering if I would be acceptable, then happy and stimulated by the discovery of shared ideas and the enormous energy and feeling of possibilities in the still new company' (P1 129).

It was the Liberation Movement which brought Churchill into contact with the women from Monstrous Regiment (they met on an abortion march). As Churchill has commented elsewhere, 'you tend to think of your own development only having to do with yourself and it's exciting to discover it in a historical context', also noting that the higher profiling of work by women playwrights (as discussed in the McFerran interview), was linked to the growth in the 1970s of new writing, fringe theatre and feminist companies.[26] Monstrous Regiment was founded in the mid-1970s by Chris Bowler, Gillian Hanna and Mary McCusker as a response to the male bias of the theatre and an urgent need to find a 'space' in which to explore their socialist-feminist ideas and politics in theatrical practice. *Vinegar Tom* was their second production, after their inaugural tour of *Scum*, which was co-scripted by Claire Luckham and Chris Bond and set in the Paris Commune of 1871.

Vinegar Tom is set in seventeenth-century rural England, and is organized into twenty-one scenes whose dramatic action is punctuated by contemporary songs to be performed *'in modern dress'* and not as *'part of the action'* (P1 133). Looking back at the critical record of *Vinegar Tom's* reception, it is the structural movement between the seventeenth-century setting and the contemporary songs which was received as problematic in terms of dramatic form. David Zane Mairowitz's commentary on *Vinegar Tom* sets Churchill's 'new feminist dimensions' against the 'pinnacle' of plays on witchcraft, Arthur Miller's *The Crucible*.[27] Churchill's socialist-feminist critique of a persecuted community of women is judged against the classic realist form which places the tragic hero (male) as the persecuted centre of dramatic action and attention. Because Churchill does not choose to draw us into a harrowing, tragic study of a persecuted (male) individual, but, reflecting the political ethos of Monstrous Regiment's style of ensemble organization and playing, looks to a collective representation of woman-centred oppression, the scenes are dismissed as 'only sketched': the desire for 'dramatic elaboration' is seen as thwarted by the 'song interruptions'. 'The playtext', Mairowitz elaborates, 'is not strong enough to withstand the breaking of its rhythm and antagonism of the musical interludes'.[28]

Similarly, despite a positive review which concluded by declaring *Vinegar Tom* an 'impressive feminist play, and an impressive feminist theatre production', feminist critic Michelene Wandor 'spent some time on the few jarring [song] moments' partly 'because the integration of different art forms in one production are [sic] difficult and perhaps need more analysis than a straightforward either/or play/musical'.[29] However, other commentators were able to take Wandor's 'either/or' query further, and to grasp that Churchill's experimentation with form did not represent a failed attempt to write in a canonical (male) tradition but was a way of exploring the possibilities of a feminist aesthetic. Commenting on the production of *Vinegar Tom*, Ned Chaillet claimed that the company had 'found a style which demands our serious attention'.[30] Gillian Hanna explained how this 'style' was a response to breaking down conventions of dramatic form, stating that 'we knew that we had to have the music to smash that regular and acceptable theatrical form', in the interests of exploring what she identified as a 'counter-cultural', feminist style of performance.[31]

The challenge to form, the 'unfixing' of boundaries, are now widely recognized strategies of feminist theatre which explore the liminal in the interests of challenging the sign of Woman. Read from this perspective, the songs are a critical and crucial key to the formal and ideological work of the play. As they are to be performed out of character and in modern dress, they create the opportunity for the performer to insert her body into the performance text as a si[gh]te of disruption. This is more than an oversimplistic linking of past and present, as Wandor argued,[32] but offers a way of representing the marginal and the absent in dominant systems of representation.

The first two songs, for example, 'Nobody Sings' and 'Oh Doctor', are specifically concerned with the invisibility of women represented by the sign of Woman. 'Nobody Sings' references the menstruating body and the cycle of the ageing body whose 'cunt' becomes 'sore and dry' in old age (P1 142). Women are 'nobody' when they are young and attractive (because objectified by the gaze), and 'nobody' when they are old because ageing renders them invisible, nonrepresentable. However, the song and performer, distanced from the dramatic action, combine to create a critical space in which to see beyond the limits of representation. As French feminist Catherine Clément, writing alongside of Hélène Cixous, argues, the menstruating body signifies both 'order and disorder'; 'it is precisely in this natural periodicity that fear, terror, that which is offside in the symbolic system will lodge itself'.[33] Making the absent body of menstruating and ageing women present is a way of showing the threat which women pose to the symbolic (i.e. the dominant order); a way of 'showing the cracks in an overall system'.[34] Significant in this respect is the juxtaposition of 'Nobody Sings' with Scene Four and the *Gestus* of the farmer's wife Margery churning the butter which 'won't come' (Pl 142). The phallocentric order is disturbed by the 'unnatural' presence of the 'offside' body.

The lyrics of 'Oh Doctor' are voiced by a woman, positioned as the disempowered patient, who pleads to know what is wrong with her; asks to have her body put back together again and to be allowed a sense of herself. The song functions as a critique of mechanistic male medicine in which women are denied ownership of their bodies and cannot be represented as a whole, merely as holes which the doctor examines with his 'metal eye' (P1 150). The 'metal eye' is evocative of psychoanalyst Luce Irigaray's speculum, which the gynaecologist uses to enter and to 'see' inside a woman's womb, but which is also the specular gaze of phallocentric desire, in which woman is represented as marginalized Other.[35] The song is inserted into Scene Six which depicts Betty, a middle-class young woman, diagnosed as 'hysteric', tied to a chair, and about to be bled as a means of controlling her body which is in revolt against her present (patriarchal) home and her future (patriarchal) prison, marriage. Framed around the *Gestus* of Betty's bleeding body (the act of showing Betty's relation to structures of social control), the song allows women to speak outside or beyond the male system of control in which the female body is fragmented, violated, abused and silenced.

These songs which image the subversive female body are echoed in the seventeenth-century community of women portrayed in the dramatic scenes. Alice, a young, unmarried mother, represents the sexually active body and woman as castrating figure. Scene Thirteen, for example, shows Alice 'giving' Jack, a married farmer who lusts after and blames Alice for his impotence, his penis back:

> JACK: Give it me then. Come on.
> SUSAN: Wait, she can't move, leave her alone.
> JACK: Give it me.
> *Alice puts her hand between his thighs.*
> ALICE: There. It's back.
> JACK: It is. It is back. Thank you, Alice, I wasn't sure you were a witch till then.
>
> (P1 64)

The birthing body is represented in Alice's friend Susan, who is married and is constantly either pregnant or miscarrying. The ageing body is figured through Alice's mother Joan, and the body of the hysteric is represented in the figure of Betty, the

28

middle-class woman who runs away from marriage.

Not all of the songs take the body as their focus, 'Something to Burn' (P1 154) thematizes the marginalization of oppressed groups – not just women, but also 'lunatics', 'blacks' and 'Jews'. 'If You Float' (P1 170) highlights women's situation as a 'catch-22': float and you are a witch; sink and you die anyway. The song critiques patriarchal 'logic' which manipulates sign-systems, arbitrarily inventing and re-inventing the 'signs' of Woman's 'evil' doing. In the 'logic' of this sign-system a woman who uses her knowledge and skills to help other women, like Ellen who is skilled in midwifery and practises abortion, can be (mis)-represented and condemned as a witch.

'Lament for the Witches' (P1 175) asks us to think about who are the witches now, and to what extent we may also be persecuted and scapegoated, and 'Evil Women' (P1 178–9), following the last scene, in which, in the manner of a music-hall routine, Kramer and Sprenger deliver lines from the *Malleus Maleficarum, The Hammer of Witches*, critiques the projection of evil on to women by the sexually inadequate man. This echoes Jack blaming Alice for his sexual impotence, but reiterates the point in a modern context. This is the contemporary man who sees 'evil women' on the 'movie screen' or in his 'own wet dream' (P1 178). Gillian Hanna explains that some spectators were critical of the play, or more specifically the songs, for constantly making parallels between the past and present, but she argues that the performers felt it was politically necessary:

> We had a very real feeling that we didn't want to allow the audience to get off the hook by regarding it [*Vinegar Tom*] as a period piece, a piece of very interesting history. Now a lot of people felt their intelligence was affronted by that. They said: 'I don't know why these people have to punctuate what they are saying by these modern songs. We're perfectly able to draw conclusions about the world today from historical parallels.' Actually, I don't believe that and, in any case, we can't run that risk. For every single intelligent man who can draw the parallels, there are dozens who don't. It's not that they can't. It's that they won't.[36]

In the seventeenth-century scenes, those women who are most marginalized in the community, because of their 'outsider' status and their lack of material status within the patriarchal and capitalist economy, are the most persecuted, and the most at risk. Alice, for example, is representative of the economically deprived single-mother group. She is separated from her child while witch-finder Packer tries to make her confess to being a witch:

PACKER: Why won't you confess and make this shorter?...
ALICE: ...I want my boy.
PACKER: Then you should have stayed at home at night with him and not gone out after the devil.
ALICE: I want him.
PACKER: How could a woman be a filthy witch and put her child in danger?
ALICE: I didn't.
PACKER: Night after night, it's well known.
ALICE: But what's going to happen to him? He's only got me.
PACKER: He should have a father...

(P1 171)

Packer's cross-examination of Alice bears a frightening resemblance to the 1990s crusade against 'lone mothers' and 'home alone' children by right-wing politicians who, for example, have argued that it is '"good Christian doctrine" to stop single women having children before they...formed stable relationships', or have 'defended the Government's right to speak out against the impact of single parenthood on crime and social breakdown.'[37] Another example, perhaps, of Churchill 'anticipat[ing] crucial issues'?

Those women in *Vinegar Tom* who are either materially better off, like Betty, and/or whose status is sanctioned by marriage, like Margery and Susan, are also victims of a male-dominated society, and are particularly oppressed by the social construct of the family, as highlighted in the song 'If Everybody Worked as Hard as Me' (P1 159–60). The *Gestus* of Scene Nineteen, Margery offers her prayer of thanks to God, the Father, while Joan and Ellen are hanged, effectively critiques the prisonhouse of religion ('you have shown your power in destroying the wicked'), patriarchy ('Bless Miss Betty's marriage and let her live happy') and capitalism ('Bless Jack...and give us the land') (P1 174).

Writing the songs for *Vinegar Tom* was a new experience for Churchill, but the ethos of feminist collectives encouraged and supported that acquisition of new skills. Churchill went on to write more songs for another Monstrous Regiment production: *Floorshow* (1977). *Floorshow* was scripted between Churchill, Bryony Lavery, Michelene Wandor and David Bradford, and used the cabaret form to tackle women's rights issues such as sexism and sexual division of labour. It was a question of raising feminist issues and politicizing theatrical form:

> We saw women acting as comperes and cracking bitterly funny jokes, and men talking about their own sexism: women refusing to act the ventriloquist's dummy, and men singing about stereotypical nursery rhymes and minding the baby.[38]

Looking back at *Owners* and forward to *Vinegar Tom*, it is possible to see how important the experience of working with the feminist company Monstrous Regiment was to the emergent 'woman writer'. Moreover, we begin to see how feminist concerns were moving to a more central position in Churchill's work during the 1970s as evidenced in her 1979 staging of sexual politics: *Cloud Nine*.

PERFORMING GENDER: *CLOUD NINE*

In between beginning and finishing *Vinegar Tom* for Monstrous Regiment, Churchill began her first workshop with director Max Stafford-Clark and the Joint Stock company with whom she was to establish an important and enduring working relationship. *Light Shining in Buckinghamshire*, detailed in the following chapter, was their first collaborative venture. *Cloud Nine*, Churchill's second production for Joint Stock, came about because Churchill and Max Stafford-Clark wanted to do another show together. As Churchill explained in an interview, she did not at first conceive of sexual politics, the topic she really wanted to work on, as a Joint Stock project:

> Joint Stock at that point was such a male company...It seemed the last company which you would think of doing a show like that, and of course as soon as I had said that, we realized that was a very good reason for in fact doing it.[39]

The 'offside' body which disrupts the symbolic in *Vinegar Tom* is a key focus in the sexual politics of *Cloud Nine* which takes the body as a critical si[gh]te of gender representation. It is written in two acts: the first uses a colonial setting to critique the Victorian values of Empire and family; the second traces the characters from Act One to a London setting in 1979, although the time shift for the characters is only twenty-five years. The continuity of linear history is, therefore, displaced by a historical memory of sexual politics; the past is physically marked in and on the body of the performer, present.

Cross-gender and cross-racial casting, and the doubling of roles are techniques central to Churchill's destabilizing of fixed sexual identities determined by dominant heterosexual ideology. The theatrical device of cross-dressing in *Cloud Nine* has been of particular interest to feminist theatre scholarship. As Sue-Ellen Case and Jeanie K. Forte, looking to examples of a 'new feminist theater practice' located in the 'critique of the self', explain, *Cloud Nine* uses the colonial setting and cross-gender casting to show a 'world of alternative identities and practices while demonstrating the link between dominant ideology and institutionalized gender roles and sexuality'.[40] The ideological pleasure of cross-dressing in *Cloud Nine* is that it allows the spectator the possibility of seeing beyond 'institutionalized gender roles and sexuality' by crossing vestimentary signs of masculinity and femininity with the 'wrong' body. This is demonstrated in the opening sequence as the patriarch, Clive, introduces his family gathered around the flagpole displaying the Union Jack: Betty his wife, 'man's creation', is played by a man; Edward his son is played by a woman; his Black man servant, Joshua, is played by a white actor, and Victoria, his daughter, represented by a doll, is, like her governess and Clive's mother-in-law, not important enough to be properly introduced (P1 251–2). Although the characters, oppressed by the imperialist roles assigned to them by Clive, affirm their identities linguistically, consenting to their given roles as what they 'want to be', visually their 'offside' bodies disrupt the construction of sexual and, in the case of Joshua, racial identities.

The tension between the 'fixing' and 'unfixing' of gender construction structures the comic play of Act One, and climaxes in the farcical 'heterosexual' marriage ceremony (a ritual conventionally used in dramatic comedy to mark the restoration of family values), between the explorer Harry, who is gay, and the governess, Ellen, who is a lesbian. Both Harry and Ellen are 'offside' bodies in the symbolic which have to be 'corrected'. Homosexuality is viewed as 'a disease more contagious than diphtheria' (P1 283), and Clive advocates marriage for Harry as a 'cure' – just as Dr Hodge 'cures' his patients and friends through aversion therapy in *Lovesick*. Harry, therefore, is to be 'cleansed' of his homosexuality and to be made safe to society through marriage.

As a lesbian, Ellen is not visible. Although Clive listens to Joshua's gossip about the possibility of an affair between Harry and Betty, he will not acknowledge the possibility of Ellen making love to his wife (P1 285). When Ellen kisses and declares her love to Betty, what the spectator sees is a man (Betty) kissing a woman (Ellen) (P1 271). Churchill's cross-gendering device highlights the visibility of heterosexuality, marking the invisibility of lesbian identity and desire.

Similarly, although Mrs Saunders, a neighbouring widow who seeks protection from Clive when the 'natives' are restless, is a heterosexual woman, as a woman on her own she poses a threat to the family unit and, like Ellen, must also be expelled. (Interestingly, in the original Joint Stock production these two roles were played by the same actress.) The Victorian double standard of sexual morality is critiqued as Clive, who continually lusts after Mrs Saunders, is imaged under her skirt having sex with her at the Christmas picnic, as voices off-stage encode the values of family and Empire in the singing of a Christmas carol (P1 263–4). Mrs Saunders dislikes Clive but, in keeping with her spirit of independence, does enjoy sex. However, there is no sexual gratification for her in an act which centres purely on Clive's climax and ejaculation. While Clive hurriedly 'comes' and rushes ('all sticky') to rejoin his family, Mrs Saunders is left asking 'What about me?' (P1 264). In her recent theorizing of a 'corporeal feminism', Elizabeth Grosz has analysed the 'come' or 'ejaculation shot' in pornography not as an imaging of male pleasure, but as a masculine fantasy of female pleasure:

> Pornography, at least in part, offers itself to the (male) spectator as a form of knowledge and conceptual/perceptual mastery of the enigmas of female sexuality but is in fact his own projection of sexual pleasure. The come shot is thus no longer an unmediated representation and demonstration of his pleasure (as one would

expect): it becomes an index of his prowess to generate her pleasure. His sexual specificity is not the object of the gaze but remains a mirror or rather a displacement of her pleasure (or at least his fantasy of her pleasure).[41]

Churchill's 'ejaculation shot', or tableau, creates a *Gestus* which indexes the wider social context in which female pleasure is displaced by the male fantasy of female sexuality and desire. This is underlined in verbal play, as Clive mistakes Mrs Saunders's unsatisfied pleasure for a 'voracious' sexual appetite, and through the visual comedy of Clive climaxing underneath the skirt of a disappointed Mrs Saunders. The Victorian skirt functions as a sign of the socially constructed feminine (especially foregrounded in the case of the 'man-made' Betty), which displaces female desire and keeps the female body (and pleasures of the body) hidden from view.

That the 'desired' purification of Harry and Ellen in Act One will not be achieved, is signalled in the closing moments of their wedding ceremony at the end of the act, when the artifice of the occasion is exposed, or literally blown away, as Joshua shoots Clive. The shooting of Clive by his Black servant is a further indication of how the violent colonization of Black skins forced into white, 'pure' masks, in turn leads to acts of violence (as dramatized in *The Hospital*.) But it especially underlines the dangers of enforcing heterosexual identity and desire. As feminist drama scholar Susan Carlson explains:

> In this parody of the typical comic happy ending, Churchill reiterates her act-long critique of social and comic tradition. Clive's celebration of the marriage – the speech with which the act ends – is, after the exposures of the act, no longer just farcical but dangerous...
>
> In exposing the empire in this Wildean fashion, she also makes tangible the danger of our consenting to the traditional stereotypes and patterns of comedy. On our road to the predictable comic ending, where are we left, when types exist only in perverted forms and when emotions find expression only clandestinely?[42]

As in *Lovesick*, the pleasure for the spectator – or, in the case of the radio play, the listener – lies in the explosion of heterosexual strait-jacketing; the *jouissance* of the marginal or 'unnatural' body disturbing, disrupting, and destroying the sexual 'norm'.

Like the characters in the play, the performers involved in

workshopping *Cloud Nine* also had to confront their own sexual prejudices and ways in which they had encountered or been oppressed by sexual stereotyping, and so on. Actor Antony Sher explains:

> Throughout the workshop we each took turns to tell our own life stories and to answer questions on our sexual experiences and lifestyles. It was nervewracking to contemplate (and far more revealing than stripping naked would have been) and so it is to the credit of the group that these sessions became the most exhilarating of all. Through them the real meaning of sexual politics was becoming clear. Each of us was secure in our separate territory male, female, gay, straight, married, single, or whatever; brainwashed by different upbringings and prejudices. However liberal we each previously thought ourselves, we were now face to face with 'the others' and so many preconceptions were proving to be wrong.[43]

Churchill has also explained how the Victorian setting for Act One reflected the way in which the actors felt that they had been brought up with Victorian attitudes which they had to rebel against in their own lives:

> When we discussed our backgrounds it occurred to us it was as if everyone felt they had been born almost in the Victorian age. Everyone had grown up with quite conventional and old-fashioned expectations about sex and marriage and felt that they themselves had had to make enormous break-aways and leaps to change their lives from that. That was why it was an appropriate image for that to set the people's childhoods in Victorian times.[44]

Although the 1970s setting for Act Two implies a more liberal time period than the Victorian past, characters are still seen to be struggling with gender roles and identities: they still have a number of prejudices and preconceptions to explore. The violence of the colonial setting (actual and metaphorical) is alluded to again through reference to the struggles in Northern Ireland (see *P1* 291, 303, 310–11). Churchill explained how they 'looked at England's relation to Ireland and how it is like a male/ female relationship'. 'The traditional view of the Irish' she continued 'is that they're charming, irresponsible, close to nature, all the things that people tend to think about women'.[45]

If Clive failed to give Mrs Saunders pleasure, then Martin, the 'new man' married to Victoria (the doll in Act One), under the guise of being liberated and wanting to discuss his wife's sexual pleasure, is, in reality, merely obsessed with his own sexual performance: 'My one aim is to give you pleasure. My one aim is to give you rolling orgasms like I do other women. So why the hell don't you have them?' (P1 300–301). Just as Mrs Saunders struggled to find ways of managing her life independently, Victoria too is trying to work out her sexuality and to consider a career move which means working away from her child, sexual partners and immediate family.

The actress who played Ellen and Mrs Saunders in Act One now takes on the role of Lin, a single lesbian mother, in love with Victoria. From being a lesbian who looked after someone else's children, Ellen, as Lin, now has a child of her own, and the possibility of a lesbian relationship, rather than the 'safety' of heterosexual marriage. Where Ellen as a lesbian was invisible, Lin speaks her desire for women and for Victoria in particular, in a way which makes her lesbian identity visible. Edward, on the other hand, is concerned that his gay identity be kept a secret in order not to lose his job as a gardener (P1 292). As his gay relationship with Gerry breaks down, he rejects a partnered gay identity for a lesbian-identified position, choosing not to live in a couple, but to live with his sister Lin and the two children.

As in Act One, the fixing and unfixing of sexual identities, as, for example, illustrated in Edward's case, also provides a structuring device for Act Two. Thematically, it is also foregrounded in an incantation scene in which Victoria, Lin and Edward pray to a female goddess and ask her to give them back 'the history we haven't had', to 'make us the women we can't be' (P1 308). The call to the goddess of 'breasts', 'cunts', 'fat bellies and babies', 'and blood blood blood' (P1 309), invokes the absent 'offside' female body, which they need to remake desire and identity beyond the conventional ordering of sexuality.

Moving beyond the gaze of the patriarch who is now reduced to a child, as the actor who played Clive in Act One doubles as Lin's child Cathy in Act Two, is figured in the representation of Betty. Betty announces that she is leaving Clive and making a life for herself. As she renegotiates relationships with her family as part of the leaving process, she also explores her sexuality. Having been driven away from auto-eroticism by her mother when she was a child, she narrates the rediscovery of her body and her ability to give herself sexual pleasure. Within the objectified gaze of her husband her own desire was absent: 'I thought if Clive wasn't looking at me there wasn't a person there' (P1 316). Touching herself, she was fearful that her 'hand might go through space' (P1 316), but she finds her own body, her own pleasures, her own orgasm, unmediated by a male presence. Hugh Rorrison, reviewing for *Plays and Players*, argued that Julie Covington's performance as Betty 'as she probes to find the personality which Victorian marriage denied her is the strongest plea for liberal attitudes in the play'.[46] In the closing image of *Cloud Nine* Clive, stuck in the patriarchal past from Act One, enters to condemn the 'new' Betty, but his presence is displaced as he exits and Betty embraces her self from Act One. The final image of the split self uniting offers women the possibility of a subjectivity beyond the objectification of the gaze.

Churchill's dramatization of sexual politics in *Cloud Nine* foregrounds the ways in which gay identities are marginalized by heterosexuality, but does not lose sight of the ways in which women are oppressed by dominant doll-like (as suggested by Victoria) representations of femininity and the absence of female desire. Part of the play's attraction and an aspect of its uniqueness is that it manages to cover a broad spectrum of sexual politics, rather than focusing on one sexually oppressed group:

> One of the things I wanted very much to do, in *Cloud 9*...was to write a play about sexual politics that would *not* just be a woman's thing. I felt there were quite a few women's groups doing plays from that point of view. And gay groups...There was nothing that also involved straight men. Max [Stafford Clark], the director, even said, at the beginning 'Well shouldn't you perhaps be doing this with a woman director?' He didn't see that it was his subject as well.[47]

From the sexual politics in *Cloud Nine* as a 'subject' which concerns us all, Churchill turned her attention in *Top Girls* to the subject of feminism as an issue of immediate, although not exclusive, concern to women.

'US AND THEM': *TOP GIRLS*

Although *Top Girls* was staged in 1982, ten years after *Owners*, ideas for the play began in the late 1970s. Churchill recalls that as early as 1977–8 she was making notes on Dull Gret, a character from the opening dinner scene, and had also had an idea about staging a play in which a lot of women from the past have coffee with a woman in the present.[48] She was also becoming increasingly concerned about the dangers of bourgeois feminism:

> It was also that Thatcher had just become prime minister; and also I had been to America for a student production of *Vinegar Tom* and had been talking to women there who were saying things were going very well: they were getting far more women executives, women vice-presidents and so on. And that was such a different attitude from anything I'd ever met here, where feminism tends to be much more connected with socialism and not so much to do with women succeeding on the sort of capitalist ladder. All of those ideas fed into *Top Girls*.[49]

While *Vinegar Tom* caught the wave of excitement generated by the Women's Movement, *Top Girls* coincided with the moment when women needed to look more closely at the complexities of feminism; to question the 1970s politics of bonding, of sisterhood, through a politics of difference.

Top Girls opens with a celebration dinner at a restaurant for 'top girl' Marlene who has just been promoted to managing director of the employment agency she works for. Celebrating her success are the women travellers, Isabella Bird and former courtesan Lady Nijo, Dull Gret and Patient Griselda taken from a Brueghel painting and a Chaucerian tale respectively, and Joan, the female 'heresy' believed to have been pope. This assembly of women, therefore, defies the logic of historical, chronological, and spatial representation, as Churchill plays with the dramatic conventions which traditionally govern time, place and character.

After the dinner the action moves to a series of short scenes in the employment agency in which a number of women seeking jobs and promotion are interviewed by Marlene and her 'top girl' agency colleagues. Cutting across these scenes is the narrative of Angie, purportedly Marlene's niece, but who is actually Marlene's real daughter. A final act, which introduces a further time shift as it is set a year earlier than the Agency scenes, stages a hard-hitting 'us and them', class-gender-confrontation scene between Marlene and her working-class sister Joyce, who has raised Angie as her own daughter.

Top Girls explores both inter- and intra-sexual oppression. The narrative threads of the dinner party conversation are significantly marked by a discourse of intersexual oppression as the women share their experiences of being daughters, wives, mistresses and mothers. Their dialogue records both patriarchal oppression and the desire to move beyond the conventional gender divide. Just as in *Cloud Nine* the characters refuse the 'fixing' of gender roles, linguistically the women in *Top Girls* mark their rejection of being represented as the feminine 'other': Isabella gave up the confines of domestic life for travel, Nijo turned from courtesan to nun, and Joan violated the 'natural' (patriarchal) order by becoming pope. The drunken climax of the dinner scene verbally and physically enacts a violent rejection of intersexual oppression as, in parallel 'texts', Gret calls on her women neighbours to leave their 'baking or washing' to fight the 'devils' in hell, to go 'where the evil come from and pay the bastards out' (P2 82); Nijo recalls conspiring with other women to beat the Emperor; Joan spews out chunks of Latin and is sick in the corner, and even Patient Griselda protests that she had rather Walter had not put her to the test as he did. However, it is significant that these 'texts' are parallel rather than interactive. Despite Marlene's plea to Joan to shut up, and Isabella's command that everyone listen to Gret because she has been to hell (P2 82), the women are largely and self-centredly caught up in their own individual narratives. The inability to listen to and to share experiences with women, is indicative of intrasexual oppression, and underscored in this first act through Churchill's use of overlapping dialogue – a technique she had recently experimented with in her short play *Three More Sleepless Nights*.[50]

Further, as a counterpoint to the desire to exit from the scene of oppression, the feminine is verbally and visually signed on and through the body. Nijo, the courtesan, for example, describes her love of clothes, silks designed to attract and to please the Emperor, and Griselda's from-peasant-girl-toprincess narrative signifies the objectification of the feminine in the heterosexual, male gaze. Moreover, as Elin Diamond has observed, the actual costuming of each of these 'top girl' women in the dinner scene 'points to the elaborate historical text that covers her body', marking the 'cost' of 'hav[ing] entered Western representation'.[51] Rejection of the masculine is, therefore, constantly warring with the physical and verbal registers of patriarchal oppression. This is further indexed in the constant juxtaposition of emotional opposites, such as laughter and misery (the women laugh at Joan, the pregnant Pope, but are moved to silence as she announces she was stoned to death at the birth of her baby, P2 71), and the 'unfixing' of the significant and the insignificant (Isabella recalls the death of her father and in the same breath places an order from the menu, P2 58).

The 'cost' of 'Western representation' is clearly encoded in the figure of Marlene, the one main character from the present (there is also the waitress), a woman who, like Marion in *Owners* is constructed as the 'conventional man'. Her identification with dominant, masculine values is reflected in the way in which actress and role are constant, unlike the 'unfixing' strategies encoded in the doubling of other characters. The figure of Marlene demonstrates how the acceptance and 'success' of a woman in the workplace requires very careful self-presentation. Like Isabella who 'always travelled as a lady', Marlene takes care not to wear trousers in the office (P2 62). The projection of a 1980s 'Superwoman' image as dramatized in the office scenes, demonstrates a need for adept role playing between high-powered lady and ball-breaking boss. Power-dressing role play does not, however, include representation of the maternal. Children and a career in a man's world are mutually exclusive, as is powerfully illustrated in Pope Joan's narrative of being stoned to death for birthing a baby, and Marlene's relationship, or rather absence of a relationship, with her daughter.

Critics have sometimes questioned the ideological purpose of Marlene, or *Top Girls* in general, asking whether to read Marlene and the play as a celebration of women's achievements or a critique of bourgeois feminism? A rather confused John Russell Taylor, for example, asked of Marlene 'well is she a heroine or isn't she?', and summed up the play as one 'which sends you out asking questions and trying to work out, not disagreeably, just what it is you have been watching'.[52] However, Marlene's male-identified subject positioning is an unequivocal indexing of Churchill's critique of bourgeois feminism. While the doubling and overlapping techniques suggest fragmentation and the possibility of 'unfixing', Marlene's stable positioning functions as an oppressive 'block' to the desires and aspirations of other women. This is especially true of her positioning in relation to Angie's narrative.

Structurally, *Top Girls* has either been presented as two acts, as in the original production, played with one interval, or as a three-act drama, played with two intervals. Churchill states her own preference for the three-act version which she claims makes the 'structure clearer: Act One, the dinner; Act Two, Angie's story; Act Three, the year before' (P2 54). As Churchill clarifies, the three-act structure underlines Angie's 'story' as the focus of the second act. This refuses an interpretation of the office scenes as a celebration of Marlene, the achiever in the workplace, by positioning the underachiever, Angie, shown in her back yard at home and as a visitor to the office, as the focus of the act and the key site of intrasexual oppression. This is visually represented in Angie wearing a dress bought for her by Marlene which is now too small for her (P2 98). The dress signifies the 'misfit' or gap between Angie's desire to be like the (well-dressed), career woman Marlene, and Marlene's dismissal of her own daughter's career aspirations as a 'packer in Tesco more like' (P2 120).

Unlike the voices of the middle-class women which dominate the linguistic space, 'dull' Angie, like Gret in Act One, is relatively silent. (Significantly, in the original Royal Court production the roles of Angie and Gret were doubled by one actress.) In Act Two Scene Two, Angie struggles to hold her own in the verbal power-play of teenage rivalry between herself and her younger, but brighter, friend Kit:

ANGIE: You know the kitten?
KIT: Which one?
ANGIE: There only is one. The dead one.
KIT: What about it?
ANGIE: I heard it last night.
KIT: Where?

ANGIE: Out here. In the dark. What if I left you here in the dark all night?

KIT: You couldn't. I'd go home.

ANGIE: You couldn't.

KIT: I'd / go home.

ANGIE: No you couldn't, not if I said.

KIT: I could.

(P2 89)

However, linguistically, Angie repeatedly fails to assert authority over Kit. Like the disempowered interviewees at the agency, she is no match for her brighter friend who sees a future for herself as a nuclear physicist. Angie's silenced, sleeping presence in the office scene at the close of the act, as Marlene verbalizes her destiny in the line, 'she's not going to make it (P2 120), prefigures her waking-nightmare state at the close of the play as, in Marlene's presence, she delivers the final, one-word line, 'Frightening' (P2 141).

Churchill's socialist-feminist critique of bourgeois-feminist values is highlighted in the final act which stages the class confrontation between the two sisters. Joyce, as the working-class mother-figure who has taken care of Angie, is represented as economically, socially and culturally 'deprived', relative to Marlene's 'top girl' success. But the devalued mothering of a child which is not her own (rather like Alec in *Owners* who saves a baby who 'belongs' to someone else) calls into question the value placed on Marlene's 'childless' career. As Sue-Ellen Case summarizes: 'the economic situation has created two choices for women: the relative economic poverty of child-rearing, or the emotional alienation of success within the structures of capitalism'.[53]

Churchill's representation of Marlene and Joyce is echoed in Isabella's narrative of her sister Hennie. As the first guest to arrive at Marlene's dinner party, Isabella's opening conversation centres on Hennie and she is quick to ask Marlene whether she, too, has a sister (P2 55). Like Marlene and Joyce, Isabella and Hennie were separated by geography. Isabella would leave for months at a time on her exotic foreign travels, returning to Hennie who stayed put in Tobermory, Scotland.[54] However, where Isabella was devoted to her sister and sustained communication through letter writing about her travels (P2

65), Marlene's obsession with her career means she hardly sees her sister, or her daughter. In Act Three it is established that Marlene has not visited Joyce and Angie for six years (P2 135). Unlike Hennie, all that Joyce and Angie receive while Marlene is away in America is the clichéd wish-you-were-here postcard which Angie treasures (P2 129).

The travel discourse of Isabella (and Nijo) illustrates how geographic mobility relates to independence. Similarly, while Marlene has enjoyed working in America and now has the excitement of running the agency in London, Joyce remains trapped in their home town (the 'back yard' setting of Act Two Scene Two suggests a working-class, terraced, urban setting), with few employment opportunities for women. Women seeking jobs through the employment agency also equate travel with career opportunities: Jeanine would like to travel (P2 86), and Shona fantasizes about an expensive car and high-powered selling up and down the M1 (P2 117). Angie's trip to London to see her 'aunt' is also her travel adventure which expresses a desire for change. However, Joyce, Angie, and the young women seeking jobs are blocked both intrasexually by the middle-class career women, and intersexually, by educational, familial and economic factors which keep them geographically and socially bound to their milieu and class, a point which Churchill would develop centrally in her next play, *Fen* (see chapter 4).

Although some spectators and critics, like John Russell Taylor, may have been confused by the formal and ideological purpose of Marlene and *Top Girls*, for others, and for women especially, it provided intense pleasures. *Top Girls* specifically, and Churchill's woman-centred, feminist theatre generally, pleasures the (feminist) spectator through the dynamics of dramatic composition and political content. As Joseph Marohl argues in an introduction to Churchill's theatre and an analysis of *Top Girls*, 'what the audience experiences during the performance, then, is defamiliarization of the ordinary (alienation effect) and the subversion of positive ideologues about gender, social hierarchies, and chronology'.[55] In contrast to some first-wave feminist drama which concentrated on the political at the expense of the theatrical, Churchill pleasured her (feminist) spectator through theatrical style and her representation of gender issues. As Gillian Hanna's comments on *Vinegar Tom* illustrated, experimenting with form is a way of representing women's (absent) experiences; of exploring the possibilities of a 'counter-cultural' aesthetics. This was exciting for women performers, spectators and, subsequently, feminist theatre scholars who, in the 1980s, became increasingly interested in the theorization of a possible feminist performance style and aesthetics.

Top Girls affords a further pleasure for the female spectator in so far as it represents an all-female community, played by an all-female cast. Creating a women-only stage picture was not uncommon in alternative feminist theatre-making in the 1970s and early 1980s. For example, the Women's Theatre Group which, like Monstrous Regiment, was established in the mid-1970s, made it a company policy to perform plays with only roles for women. In a mainstream context, however, women-only plays tended to succeed on mainstream terms, which is not surprising given, as McFerran's interview with the women playwrights demonstrated, the male domination of theatre. For example, Nell Dunn's all-female cast (with the exception of one unseen male presence) in her commercially successful play *Steaming*, performed shortly before *Top Girls* in 1981, and which sets the women in a Turkish bath, combines a bourgeois-feminist position with the dominant form of stage realism. By contrast, *Top Girls* exceptionally combines theatrical inventiveness with a more hard-hitting, radical political viewpoint which, rather than support mainstream, bourgeois feminism, takes issue with it.

From a socialist-feminist viewpoint the spectatorial experience of *Top Girls* is an important one. As feminist historian Rosalind Miles, commenting on the major British revival of *Top Girls* in 1991, observed and cautioned:

> Superb parts for women then, written by women – watching this on International Women's Day, a moment here and there felt like a new dawn. And yet. How much has changed for women in the theatre in the last nine years? Or in life? In *Top Girls*, the women trapped in traditional roles face a cruelly bleak future.[56]

The future remains as 'cruelly bleak' for those women in the 1990s as it did in the Thatcherite years of the 1980s, which were 'stupendous' for one class, but not for another. The need for Churchill's socialist-feminist critique of class and gender issues is arguably, therefore, all the more critical in the current backlash[57] climate of the 1990s when even the acceptable face of bourgeois feminism is under threat.

With *Cloud Nine*, Churchill achieved transatlantic and commercial success. *Top Girls*, similarly, was acclaimed in Britain and America. Both plays won Obie awards and went on to be performed around the world.[58] Churchill's success – and continued success – is due in part to her willingness to experiment (see chapter 5). In *Top Girls*, for example, it was the pleasure of the overlapping dialogue, additional to the techniques of doubling and time-shifting that she 'played' with in *Cloud Nine*, which caught the critical attention. Paying tribute to Churchill, Gillian Hanna has described her as 'the only woman I know of who has managed to keep herself at a level of enquiry...into the aesthetic process. She is constantly re-writing herself'.[59] The innovative approach of the 'woman writer' to theatre-making, the ability to 'constantly re-writ[e] herself', has secured Churchill a place not only in the canon of contemporary women's theatre which, regretfully, continues to occupy a marginal position in relation to dominant theatre and culture, but also in the 'malestream' of the modern British stage.[60]

3

The Dramatist as
Socialist Critic

> I think labels and terms like feminist writer or woman writer or left-
> wing writer vary very much ... depending on who's using them and
> why ... I think I only mind it in any sense at all – and mostly I would
> embrace it as being a reasonably accurate description – ... if you
> think that in the other person's mind that conveys something very
> narrow or specific which doesn't really cover the breadth of your
> work, or that it conveys with it a stereotype of the kinds of things
> that they expect that you'll be writing.[1]

Churchill has identified 'two obsessions' in her early work: one,
which was the focus of the opening chapter, was concerned with
'mental states, lovesickness, schizophrenia, and so on', and the
other was an 'anticapitalist, state of England sort of thing', usually
in a rather negative and sad mode'.[2] *The Ants*, Churchill's first
professional radio production (1962), described as 'the most
successful of these political plays',[3] illustrates this second
obsession.

The Ants uses a familial setting to dramatize an estranged set
of parents arguing over the custody of their son, Tim, who is
temporarily staying with his grandfather until marital dishar-
mony and living arrangements are resolved. As a refuge from
parental quarrelling, Tim focuses on a community of ants, but as
tempers flare he turns on the ants, and, finally, joins his
grandfather in setting fire to them:

> Pour a little petrol on them, that's right. Now we put the string here
> in the petrol and bring the end way over here so we can shelter from
> the blast all right? Down we crouch, then, oh. Now we light the
> string, here, see, light the string. [*He strikes a match.*] You take the
> match, you do it. That's right. Blow out the match. Now you wait, the

string will burn all the way down to the enemy, see the little flame go all the way down to the ants.[4]

The radio play ends with the directions *'the petrol explodes into flame'* and Tim *'shrieks with laughter'*.[5] Metaphorically, the burning of the ants is designed to express the horrors of war, and the ways in which people (Tim) can switch from identifying with a community of people (the ants) to bombing (setting fire to) them. In this context, the damaging (emotionally violent) familial relationships are seen to give rise to an act of violence.

During the 1970s, the early political impulse of a piece like *The Ants* can be seen evolving in Churchill's dramatizations of an anti-capitalist stance, the exploration of violent actions, and strategies of social control and resistance. These emerge alongside, or, rather, are integral to the concerns of the 'woman writer'. As the opening quotation suggests, 'left-wing' and 'feminist' are both labels frequently used to describe Churchill's writing. Where the previous chapter foregounded Churchill as a feminist playwright, the purpose of this chapter is to look more closely at formative work which has contributed to her reputation as a left-wing writer; to bring her emergent role as socialist critic into focus.

'TERRORISM AND SEASIDE': *OBJECTIONS TO SEX AND VIOLENCE*

The issue of bombing, alluded to in *The Ants*, was one which Churchill returned to in her mid-1970s stage play *Objections to Sex and Violence* (1975). *Objections to Sex and Violence* was her next full-length production at the Court after *Owners*, although, before then, she had completed the writing of another play, *Moving Clocks Go Slow*, a science-fiction drama given a one-night performance later in 1975 in the Royal Court Theatre Upstairs.[6] Performed on the Court's main stage, *Objections to Sex and Violence* raised, as Churchill explained in her afterword to the play, published ten years after its production, 'immediate and pressing ideas about the anarchism, revolution and violence' in Britain in the early 1970s. She added that many of the IRA bombings had not happened at the time she wrote the piece, although 'it's hard to unthink them and see the play without them' (*OSV* 52).

Violence as an act of insurrection on the part of the individual is dramatized in the representation of the central female character, Jule. In Act One it is established that Jule has been living among a small group of agitators who are apparently prepared to use violence in protests against society. Although there are vague references to capitalism, revolution, and explosive devices, particular political affiliations, causes and the exact nature of intended violence are never clearly established. Reviewer Harold Hobson opined that the 'play's foundation ... is the power, and especially the obscurity of the motives of violence'.[7]

The dramatic action is set on a beach where Jule and Eric, also a group member, are living in a tent following police raids and arrests made on conspiracy charges.[8] The issue of violence or more specifically objections to it, are raised through the dialogue between Jule, her sister Annie, and Annie's boyfriend Phil. Out of concern for Jule's safety, Annie and Phil have come looking for her at the seaside:

> JULE: What did you come for?
> ANNIE: You sent me a postcard.
> JULE: I didn't say come. I was keeping in touch.
> ANNIE: I read about the trouble in the paper, but when I took a train up you'd vanished. You weren't just out because I waited all day. The police said they hadn't kept you.
> JULE: It's not my fault you waited all day. I can't always be where you might drop in.
> ANNIE: So when I knew from the postmark you were here, I came here, that's all.

> (*OSV* 13)

Jule's subversive position in relation to violence is the catalyst for debating the morality of violent actions, and for looking at the violence people are subjected to in their everyday lives. Some of the most poignant moments in Act One, for example, centre on the gradual unfolding of Annie's story about her private and public life, at home and at work, which includes detail of a violent, past marriage and her inability to cope with her job as a secretary. Annie's monologue describing her work experience is a precursor to the narratives of disempowerment voiced by the interviewees in the *Top Girls* agency:

> I was secretary to a top executive. But you know how it is. I go to pieces. They bust me down to the typing pool for a rest, they were quite concerned. That's when I should have left. But I like to feel committed. I don't know how to keep my distance. I bring my work home in my head as if it was interesting. As if I was competing like the men. You'd love the men, Jule, you'd laugh so much. You can tell the grade of a man by his car. The company provide them with different sizes so there's no mistaking who's important. (*OSV* 14)

Annie goes on to tell how she switched from office work to cleaning for her former boss, whom she admits to blackmailing after he desired to have sex with her on a regular basis. The day before coming away to find Jule, Annie had told her boss it was all over: 'I'm sick of blackmailing you all this time, it makes me feel ill' (*OSV* 25). He, however, then revealed that his wife had known about them all along, and had agreed to the sex and to the money. Annie's fantasy of being less of a victim of feeling that she 'was doing something to them' is destroyed:

> I really thought I was doing something to them. I used to feel good cleaning up her shit because I thought I knew what was what and she'd got no idea. When really I was the one. That's all it is. Whatever you do to them, they can afford it, they include it, they glide. That's all it is that makes me cry. (*OSV* 26)

Although Jule tries to incite Annie to violent retaliation, suggesting a brick through the couple's window, Annie is forced to admit that, unlike her sister, she is unable to occupy an 'extreme position' (*OSV* 26).

Incitement to and resistance of subversive attitudes to sex and violence create the tensions in the drama, as Jule tries to persuade those around her of her views. Although the play is conventionally organized into two acts, there are moments when Churchill shows signs of experimenting with a more Brechtian style to demonstrate the issues of sex and violence as, for example, in the close of Act One when Annie, Jule and Phil are all roused to anger over the behaviour of Annie's employer. As in *The Ants*, lighting a fire creates a *Gestus* for upset, resentment and anger, and Jule's final line of the act, addressed to Annie, invites her not to 'turn away from it' (*OSV* 33). Similarly, Jule's anger with Eric in the second act, as he reveals he has half-promised the police information on the group members and is going to leave altogether in order to keep his silence, is imaged in the throwing of sand, and then the throwing of stones which becomes increasingly more violent and threatening.

After Eric retreats from the scene, Jule begins to bury herself in the sand, and, subsequently, Annie takes up the task of burying her sister until only her head is left showing. Reviewer W. Stephen Gilbert, while critiquing the play for its lack of 'visual realisation of the verbal motifs' described this 'decapitation' sequence as 'the most theatrical image of the evening':

> Annie has rendered Jule a talking head by burying her up to the neck in the sand, as she used to do in childhood. Mocked for her threat of violence, she stuffs sand in Jule's mouth and flounces off. The image is a small miracle of compression and evocation. Jule is, as it were, raped and murdered.[9]

Ultimately, although Jule is able to incite those around her to momentary anger they counter with objections of reasonableness. It becomes impossible, therefore, for Jule to establish a group dedicated to revolutionary violent action. One of Churchill's sources for *Objections to Sex and Violence* was Hannah Arendt's *On Violence* (*OSV* 52). In her study, Arendt, quoting from Frantz Fanon, explains the bonding which underpins 'collective violence':

> We find a kind of group coherence which is more intensely felt and proves to be a much stronger, though less lasting, bond than all the varieties of friendship, civil or private. To be sure, in all illegal enterprises, criminal or political, the group, for the sake of its own safety, will require 'that each individual perform an irrevocable action' in order to burn his bridges to respectable society before he is admitted into the community of violence.[10]

What Churchill shows in her drama is that neither Annie, Phil, Eric, nor Terry, Jule's estranged husband who turns up at the close of Act Two, can commit themselves to an 'irrevocable' violent action which would bind them to Jule's position and to a 'community of violence'.

Interwoven with this serious discussion of violence are scenes depicting 'the seaside couple Madge and Arthur' which are in a lighter comic vein (*OSV* 52). In her notes Churchill found a topical reference to the couple as follows: 'Mary Whitehouse and man in raincoat as married couple – both with same ashamed attitude to sex – they think of themselves as different but in fact identical' (*OSV* 52). In the early 1970s, objections to sex, or rather to representations of sex, were being raised by, for example, Mary Whitehouse's Viewers and Listeners Association, which paid fastidious attention to sex and media broadcasting, and Lord Longford's *Report on Pornography* published in 1972. Just as the other characters repress their momentary violent urges in the interests of civilized behaviour, Madge and Arthur repress sex and sexual fantasies as something shameful and disgusting, but to comic effect. Arthur, for example, lusts after Miss Forbes, another lonely, distressed figure who has come to the seaside, driven by a repressed past romantic memory. His advances towards Miss Forbes are en-acted in the postcard-cartoon style of a raincoat-flasher on the beach:

> ARTHUR: My wife disapproves of everything. I'm forced to go to shops for literature. I can't help it, it's a natural urge, it's disgusting but I can't help that. You're the same, you're no better, you dance, you've had men, you like it, you like it, you'd like it now, you want me to do it now, it's not my fault, you're making me do it, you're making me.
> *Arthur undoes his trousers.*
> touch me, quick, touch me, touch me, touch me –
> *Miss Forbes shrieks and rushes away. She trips over some rocks near the sea's edge and falls heavily.*
> *Arthur hastily does up his trousers.*
> Look what you made me do. It's not my fault. It's you. It should be stopped.
>
> (*OSV* 43)

Writing the afterword in the mid-1980s, Churchill stated that the title of her play suggested 'a different set of ideas, developed by feminists, of the links between male sexuality and violence, which wasn't my starting point at all' (*OSV* 52). This was a line of interpretation, however, which inflected Irving Wardle's (critical) reviewing of the original production, stating as he did that 'we are back in the traditional feminine world where personal relation-ships are all and everything would work out satisfactorily if men would only behave properly'.[11] 'With the possible exception of Terry, the communist husband', he continues, 'each of the men makes his exit with a knife from the author quivering between the shoulder blades'.[12] These comments, however, say more about the

51

male bias and attitude of the reviewer than they do about the play. Although Churchill places a woman centre stage as the active protagonist, surrounded by relatively passive men (as she does, for example with Marion in *Owners*) there is little in the text of the drama itself to support the radical-feminist, anti-male position Wardle reads into the production.

Although the title may, as Churchill writing in 1985 suggested, signal issues of male-authored violence against women, a more topical concern for a revival of the play in the 1990s would probably be the relationship of women to violence. This has proved a controversial issue for feminism, as plays and films such as *My Sister in this House* (1981), *A Question of Silence* (1982), or, more recently, *Thelma and Louise* (1991) and *Lesbians Who Kill* (1992), have shown, and is one which Churchill would explore in her mid-1980s play, *A Mouthful of Birds* (see Chapter 5).

Meanwhile, not all critics were as severe as Wardle. Harold Hobson wrote that the 'English Stage Company has acquired a dramatist of an exceptionally high order',[13] and although W. Stephen Gilbert had reservations about *Objections to Sex and Violence*, he concluded his review by favourably comparing Churchill with the established left-wing, political writer, Edward Bond:

> It [*Objections to Sex and Violence*] reminds me at times of the work of Edward Bond, by which I mean the highest praise. The sheer economy and resonance of Bond's stagecraft is unsurpassed amongst contemporary dramatists. Ms Churchill may be going to alter that assessment. At any rate, she's going to be a major dramatist.[14]

Despite this praise, I would argue that the relatively conventional structure of *Objections to Sex and Violence* and the focus on individual acts of (potential, rather than actual) insurrection make the play less interesting, both stylistically and politically, than Churchill's first Joint Stock production, *Light Shining in Buckinghamshire* (1976).

FROM HISTORY TO HISTORICIZATION: *LIGHT SHINING IN BUCKINGHAMSHIRE*

Like *Vinegar Tom*, which, as was previously noted, Churchill was writing in the same period, *Light Shining in Buckinghamshire* is set in the seventeenth century. Churchill's dramatization challenges the oversimplified version of the English civil war between Cavaliers and Roundheads by offering a more complex view of this period in English history when, in the middle part of the century, in fighting to overthrow the monarchy, it was, briefly, believed to be possible to revolutionize the oppressed lives of ordinary men and women. Politically, Churchill moves from the subversive potential of the individual without a clearly defined cause, to the rebellion of a society seeking economic and sexual freedoms, and, stylistically, shifts from realistic dialogue punctuated by stylized moments to a performance mode more fully informed by Brechtian techniques.

Light Shining in Buckinghamshire was Churchill's first encounter with Joint Stock's method of collective working. In the initial three-to-four-week period of workshopping, which was how work for a project began, the time was spent familiarizing the company with seventeenth-century history. This was rather a different experience to the subsequent *Cloud Nine* workshop, as director Max Stafford-Clark explained:

> *Light Shining in Buckinghamshire*... was about an experience very distant from us – Levellers, Ranters and ecstatic religion in the mid-17th century; the workshop brought it closer to us, made it more familiar, whereas *Cloud Nine* was about ourselves and things that were familiar to us, and the period of work actually distanced it.[15]

In the same interview, Stafford-Clark went on to argue that the writing and performance processes benefit from this kind of workshop experience, because the actors bring to it a level of 'creativity' and 'commitment' not usually demanded of them:

> Actors are often in a situation where they make the most of what they've got. Their creativity is rarely called upon. You gain their commitment if you say to them: 'The script will finally be written by the author, but first we all have an opportunity to explore our own obsessions and create things from scratch, to explore, to initiate subjects'. You're tapping a source of energy that normally plays don't demand.[16]

Just as Churchill was excited by the collaborative, feminist project with Monstrous Regiment, working with Joint Stock was also a stimulating introduction to a new way of working and a departure from her more 'solitary' life as a writer. Her write-up of the *Light Shining in Buckinghamshire* project which she contributed to Rob Ritchie's *The Joint Stock Book* recaptures the 'thrill' of this new collective process and gives an insight into the kinds of improvization techniques which Joint Stock used:

> I'd never seen an exercise or improvisation before and was as thrilled as a child at a pantomime. Each actor had to draw from a lucky dip of bible texts and get up at once and preach, urging some extraordinary course of action justified from the Bible: 'Suffer little children to come unto me' became an impassioned plea to lay children in the street and run them over with a steamroller. They drew cards, one of which meant you were eccentric to the power of that number, and then improvised a public place – a department store, a doctor's waiting room – till it gradually became clear who it was, how they were breaking conventions, and how the others reacted.[17]

Churchill took away ideas, characters and scenes suggested to her during the workshopping period with Joint Stock, mixed with historical documentary sources, such as Leveller newspapers or Digger pamphlets. Close upon the rehearsal period, however, the script was still unfinished. A further drafting and exchange of ideas precipitated a shift from her concentration on six major roles, with actors playing minor parts in each others' narratives, to the concept of there being no continuity between actors and characters from scene to scene. This was jointly arrived at between Churchill and Stafford-Clark – first as a joke and then later as an idea to be taken seriously, as Churchill explains:

> We had the idea jointly – we suggested it jokingly, and then came back to it: 'What we ought to do is let everybody play different parts, and not worry about characters going through'. That reduced the number of scenes it needed, and it made everybody's experience seem shared. In a war or a revolution the same things happen to a lot of people. We then had to put it to the actors that they weren't going to play the parts they thought they were – they were all going to share the parts.[18]

While Churchill and Stafford-Clark were anxious about how the performers might react to the demands of sharing the parts, the collective distribution of roles and the radical break with the dramatic convention of actor-character identification was also one which made demands on the spectator. In his review, Irving

Wardle drew attention to the absence of 'personal heroes or villains', and, while describing the characterization of Cromwell as 'an affable negotiator' noted, in an aside, that this was observed 'on the one occasion he appears'.[19] Working against the tradition of actor-character identification, however, was central to making the play about ordinary people, and not – as Irving Wardle may have secretly liked – a historical play about Oliver Cromwell, for example. On the contrary, as David Zane Mairowitz argued, 'the play's history is rooted wholly in a collective consciousness which is its protagonist and hero', and although Mairowitz described the interchanging of roles as 'initially...confusing', he proceeded to argue that this was both theatrically and politically necessary:

> Churchill does not feel constrained by the pre-eminence of personality in our culture (and in our theatre), and twists our comprehension of inter-relationships in her view of events and in her operation of the stage. The brilliant collective playing of Joint Stock in Max Stafford-Clark's production first makes her style seem palatable, and finally correct and necessary.[20]

Writing and playing in a democratic, socialist, performance register enabled Churchill to ask different questions of seventeenth-century history; to demonstrate what is missing in the received, schools' version of English history. By playing in the 'gaps', Churchill and Joint Stock moved from a dramatic representation of history to a Brechtian mode of historicized performance. As feminist theatre scholar Elin Diamond explains in her seminal essay on 'Brechtian Theory / Feminist Theory', 'Brechtian historicization challenges the presumed ideological neutrality of any historical reflection'.[21] Diamond elaborates:

> In historicized performance, gaps are not to be filled in, seams and contradictions show in all their roughness, and therein lies one aspect of spectatorial pleasure – when our differences *from* the past and *within* the present are palpable, graspable, applicable.[22]

The dual movement between the historical past, and the present history-in-the-making is an important one. In both *Light Shining in Buckinghamshire* and *Vinegar Tom* it is not just a question of seeing the 'gaps' in seventeenth-century history but of also seeing them 'within the present'. Commenting on Brecht's 'disgust' with realism, because of its 'hegemonic' tendencies,

Diamond further adds that 'this is perhaps why the most innovative women playwrights refuse the seamless narrative of conflicting egos in classic realism'.[23] Neither *Light Shining in Buckinghamshire* nor *Vinegar Tom* offer 'seamless narratives' of individuals; rather, they are both rooted in collective representations which unpick the seams of history. Their respective collective performance registers democratize both the playing space and the playing of history.

Focusing more specifically on the dramatic text, it is possible to see how in *Light Shining in Buckinghamshire* Churchill moves from the individual as a member of a small, anarchic group, which she dramatized in *Objections to Sex and Violence*, to staging revolution, or rather, the possibility of revolution, on a national scale. As a socialist critic, she looks at the conditions which make a revolution possible, highlighting the failing authority of the king, the challenge to the integrity of government, and the willingness of the army to use force against the Royalists. However, the play also demonstrates the reasons behind the failed revolution. In the Putney debates which bring the first act to a close, it is property, ownership, i.e. developing capitalism, which Cromwell and his supporters use to argue against enfranchisement. In Act Two the betrayal of the people continues as the army, used to fighting for equality and freedom in God's name, is now armed against the Levellers and Diggers, and is used to fight against Ireland; the oppressed are forced to fight against the oppressed. In the final 'Meeting' scene, only the Ranters, with their faith in the millennium and the coming of Christ, remain clutching their hope of revolution before the Restoration.

Each scene in Churchill's Brechtian montage is a highly charged fragment of revolutionary belief, action and failure. As Irving Wardle explained, 'it is a model of expressive brevity, each scene, no matter how powerfully charged, cut off as if by a guillotine as the actor steps out of character'.[24] Civil battles and struggles are condensed and imaged through techniques of Brechtian reporting. Actors announce or narrate events, as in the opening to Act Two, for example, which documents the crushing of the Diggers, who tried to claim and work common land for the dispossessed poor, and, later in the act, the account of the funeral of Robert Lockyer, a Leveller leader, which is read by one of the actors from a Leveller newspaper (P1 228).

One of the key ways in which Churchill makes the complexities of this revolutionary moment in history accessible to the spectator is through a recurrent imaging of the conflict between those who can afford to eat and those who are forced to go hungry. In Act One, for example, the vicar talks to his servant, Claxton, while seated at a table set with wine (which he pours only for himself) and oranges (P1 192–3). He preaches to Claxton on greed as the cause of civil unrest and personalizes his sermonizing by asking after Claxton's baby who is dangerously ill. He brings their encounter to a close by offering Claxton an orange from his table for the baby. The *Gestus* of the orange-giving, discredits his (mis)understanding of a people who fight not out of greed as he believes, but out of hunger and a need to feed their families and to raise healthy children. His final homily, 'And if it [the baby] is not spared, we must submit. We all have to suffer in this life', is undercut by the direction '*He drinks*' (P1 193). His rhetoric of godliness and caring for his parishioners is demonstrated as nothing but self-interest and self-importance.

Similarly, when the working man Briggs signs up for the army, he simply looks on while the recruiting officer, Star, from the mercantile classes, punctuates his explanation of the army's Christian purpose with eating meat (P1 198-9). Despite arguing social equality, Star reacts to the way in which Briggs marks their 'equal' standing by keeping his hat on in his presence. This, therefore, undermines the sincerity of his explanations of social and civil division, delivered in the manner of a Brechtian teaching text designed to school Briggs in the distinction between oppressors and oppressed; between Normans and Saxons, and between Royalists and the army of Christ's saints. Expanding on the culinary and biblical frame of reference used by Star, Briggs recites his lesson back to his 'teacher':

BRIGGS: Bacon. Is bacon Norman?
STAR: Pork, Briggs. Pig. Very good.
BRIGGS: And Jacob the younger brother is the Saxon herds the pigs.
    And Esau the older brother is the Norman eats the pork.
STAR: Very good, Briggs, Excellent.

(P1 199)

57

In Act Two, which strips away the possibility of revolution, being able to afford to eat is forcefully expressed in a scene showing a woman abandoning her baby because she cannot afford to feed it. This is positioned in between a scene in which Star is shown as the new landlord taking possession of the land, and proposing reforms for the so-called benefit of the poor, and a monologue in which a butcher addresses his (unseen) customers and threatens a gentleman customer who can afford to buy meat. The butcher's outburst is a violent and powerful imaging of the 'haves and have nots': 'You cram yourselves with their children's meat. You cram yourselves with their dead children' (P1 228). As rich men feed off the hunger of the poor, it is the poor and their children, and future generations of children, who are left starving. The sceptre of the child who is hungry and damaged by capitalist greed is an absent presence which haunts the action of the play (and future plays by Churchill, such as *Fen*, or, more recently still, *The Skriker*).

As the introduction of a capitalist system makes 'owners' of a few and beggars of many, it denies people the possibility of nourishment from the earth. In the final moments of *Light Shining in Buckinghamshire* the socialist dream of a more equal society is represented in the figure of Briggs, who is reduced to eating grass as he tries to balance the equation in which some eat too much by being someone who eats very little. But even when he forces his body to survive on grass alone, nevertheless, it is grass growing in a field which is owned by somebody else (P1 240).

Although gender is not a primary focus in *Light Shining in Buckinghamshire*, as it is in *Vinegar Tom*, ordinary women are shown to be more oppressed than men, both productively and reproductively. The figure of Margaret Brotherton, a displaced or dispossessed vagrant who is moved on from parish to parish, is representative of the ways in which women would increasingly have no sense of belonging in developing capitalism. In the Putney Debates it is only the enfranchisement of the common man which is debated, women are not considered. That women do not have a voice is further demonstrated when Hoskins tries to argue with the preacher who attempts to silence her with his pronouncement 'women can't speak in church' (P1 201). After Hoskins is beaten for trying to speak out, the wife of a working man tends her wounds and argues (with overtones of *Vinegar Tom*) the 'evil' and 'shameful' nature of women and their childbearing bodies as the rationalization for the silencing of women (P1 204). The invisibility of women is also highlighted in the scene 'Two Women Look in a Mirror' as the women see themselves for the first time in a mirror, left behind in the deserted house of a Royalist:

> 1ST WOMAN: There's an even bigger mirror that we didn't break. I'll show you where. You see your whole body at once. You see yourself standing in that room. They must know what they look like all the time. And now we do. (P1 207)

The possibility of working-class representation is, however, never realized – not for men, and especially not for women.

The exclusion of women from political and economic life, and the denial of sexual freedom, which women like Hoskins as a Ranter believed in, represent further 'gaps' for the feminist spectator to consider. The Women's Movement had its own war to wage on behalf of women's rights, but as Eva Figes was to caution in a revised edition of *Patriarchal Attitudes*, 'we are in danger of being lulled into a sense of premature complacency: we may have won the first battle, but we are still a long way from winning the war'.[25]

'WATCHING THE DETECTIVES': *SOFTCOPS*

Churchill continued her socialist critique in her work for television with *The After-Dinner Joke*, broadcast in 1978, which looked at capitalism and charity work.[26] The topic of terrorism and bombing surfaced again in *The Legion Hall Bombing* (1979) which took issue with the juryless Diplock Courts in Northern Ireland, and proved a controversial broadcast on account of last-minute censorship on the part of the BBC.[27] Immediately after this, Churchill worked on the scripting of *Softcops*, which she connects with *The Legion Hall Bombing* on account of the way in which both works tackle 'the depoliticization of crime, or calling things crimes that other people might call political acts'.[28]

For *Softcops*, Churchill acknowledges her debt to Foucault's *Discipline and Punish*. Taking her cue from Foucault, Churchill explores the evolution of social systems of control and punishment, and focuses on nineteenth-century France, setting the play in Paris during the 1830s. The spectator is taken through a series of scenes which explicate different methods of social control, from the spectacle of the tortured body to Bentham's Panopticon; from watching punishment to the punishment of being watched. Although Churchill wrote *Softcops* in 1978, it was not performed until Howard Davies's production of the play for the RSC in 1984. Michael Ignatieff described setting and set for the production as follows:

> *Softcops* is Foucault rendered as a music-hall turn and a Victorian freak-show, with music by Brecht and Gilbert and Sullivan. Set in the Paris of Vidocq and Lacenaire, the series of sketches is acted by an all-male company of players in dinner-jackets working on the bare boards of The Pit amid a set (by Bob Crowley) of draped mirrors, ladders doubling as gallows, tables and chairs doubling as execution blocks, and a hint of a Paris bordello in the middle distance. The Medici String Quartet plays by candle-light and offers mock-solemn musical shading for the action: a single plucked note to punctuate the silence of the Panopticon; a pizzicato in time with the boys scratching on their slates at the juvenile reformatory.[29]

By demonstrating how systems of social control operate and link up – the policing of education, punishment, mental health, and so on – Churchill shows how social behaviour is regulated and how, therefore, the power structure of government remains undiminished. Although there is no moment of revolution in *Softcops*, as dramatized in *Light Shining in Buckinghamshire*, the revolutionary impulse of *Softcops* lies in the spectator response to being shown how strategies of resistance are resisted by the enforcement of governmental power structures which seek to maintain law and social order. The spectator is, however, invited to question rather than accept the policing of social behaviour through understanding the mechanisms by which it is enforced. From the looking through to the being looked at sequences it is the spectator who is ultimately 'watching the detectives' and is empowered to interrogate the methods of 'softcop' control.

When the play was performed in 1984 it was the Panoptic principle of surveillance which caught the attention of audiences, given the association with George Orwell's 'Big Brother' (P2 3). Several of the reviewers, however, were unconvinced by and uncertain of what Churchill was attempting to portray in *Softcops*.

Criticisms varied from Rosalind Carne's damning 'one of the least enjoyable evenings I can remember in three years' regular theatre going...it keeps you guessing, and hoping, but consistently fails to provide what it promises',[30] to Michael Billington's more benign, 'I think I see what Ms Churchill is against, I am not sure what she is for'.[31]

The mode of looking in *Softcops* is directed by the figure of Pierre who functions as the spectator's link between each tableau of punishment. As the play opens, Pierre is stage-managing his organized spectacle of punishment. To an audience of invited schoolchildren he explains the theatrical sign-system of the scaffolding set for the 'performance'. As a semiotician, Pierre has worked to determine the scenic encoding and to direct and close off meanings. The impossibility of this task, however, is highlighted as he makes last-minute set changes; for example, having the red ribbons, which he wants the children to 'read' as symbols of blood and passion, removed because they intrude too much on the black of the scaffolding drape, signifying grief. Moreover, the scripting of roles which he has so carefully prepared goes wrong as his 'cast' of prisoners and local dignitaries forget their lines and have to be prompted. Pierre's performance is a complex indexing of Brechtian theatre – a performance designed to make the children think, where scenes are announced by placards (which Pierre gets wrong), and actors break the fourth wall convention, stepping in and out of character – which has dangerous consequences for the actor-prisoners who 'play' with their 'real' bodies. Ultimately, Pierre's inability to semiotically determine the meaning of his performance is demonstrated in the crowd response to the murderer Lafayette, whose refusal to deliver his rehearsed speech of contrition and his expression of pleasure in having killed his boss, incites a riot. In this brief moment of insurrection it is the crowd who becomes the performer and controls the 'spectacle'.[32] Order is restored, however, by using soldiers, indicating, as was shown in *Light Shining in Buckinghamshire,* that the allegiance of an armed force is crucial to establishing and maintaining, or to bringing down, structures of governmental power.

Brechtian styled role-playing continues in the 'cop and robber' sequence which follows, depicting Vidocq, arch villain turned Chief of Police and Lacenaire, who, as Churchill explains, was a 'glamorous and ineffectual murderer and petty thief, who was briefly a romantic hero' (P2 3). The Brechtian, multi-disguised, multiple-role-playing of Vidocq and the interchange-ability of villain and cop identities makes ambiguous the demarcation between law enforcement and criminality, while the circus-style celebration of Lacenaire is used for political ends to conceal the more dangerous figure of Fieschi, put to death for trying to kill the king (P2 32). Ideologically, this is a clear example of what Churchill wanted to show as the representation of a political act as a crime.[33] Stylistically, as one critic described, the overall effect was 'a cross between the *Marat/Sade* and the more arid Mr Bond'.[34]

Vidocq's control of crime (and it is now crimes against property which is seen as the major issue), poses a problem for Pierre. Catching criminals is all very well he admits, but what happens 'if you don't use their bodies to demonstrate the power of the law' (P2 30). Foucault asks a related question of his theoretic in *Discipline and Punish*, as he queries the framing of his study, which traces the way in which the visible body as the si[gh]te of punishment was displaced by systems of correction which addressed the unseen 'soul' of the transgressor, against a background of 'a history of bodies'. However, as the more adept semiotician, Foucault recognizes that 'even when they use "lenient" methods involving confinement or correction, it is always the body that is the issue – the body and its forces, their utility and their docility, their distribution and their submission'.[35] Moreover, it is the body as sign-system he goes on to explain, which is 'directly involved in a political field; power relations have an immediate hold upon it; they invest it, mark it, train it, torture it, force it to carry out tasks, to perform ceremonies, to emit signs'.[36] Pierre, through understanding Bentham's Panoptic principle, is eventually persuaded of the effectiveness of a system of punishment which shifts from visibility to invisibility; from the spectacle of the 'theatre' to the power 'machine' of surveillance (P2 40). Michael Ignatieff describes the theatrically effective enactment of the Panoptic principle in the 1984 production:

> Bentham explains the Panopticon. He drapes a ladder with a shroud, places a bowler hat on top of it and disappears behind. Silence

descends, the prisoner stares at the ladder, we stare at the ladder, and it begins to stare back at us. Quick as a wink, Bentham appears behind the prisoner's back, smiling benignly at his terror. It's not being watched that matters, it's thinking you're being watched.[37]

It is the *Gestus* of the marked body, however, which Churchill uses to make the repressed traces of social control visible: the children in their harnesses of physical and spiritual correction; the 'docile' bodies of the young boys in 'family' institutions of correction, and the 'rehabilitated' bodies of Pierre's hospital patients in the final scene.

Given that when performed in 1984 *Softcops* had an all-male cast, critical readings have sometimes separated this play from Churchill's emergent feminism. Jane Thomas, for example, states that 'Churchill's anonymous group of males is presumably representative of all deviations from the bourgeois norm including non-whites and women', and goes on to argue that 'gender did not constitute a focus for her [Churchill's] ideas until the late seventies'.[38] This, however, overlooks the complex interconnections of feminism and politics in Churchill's theatre in the 1970s, and, moreover, specifically negates the gender focus of *Vinegar Tom*, written in 1976 before the writing of *Softcops* in 1978.

The idea that the men in the play represent or stand in for women is, however, an important one. Janelle Reinelt, offering a different view than that of Thomas, sees the absence of women in the play as having 'profound implications for the feminist project', stating that, 'women do not have to be represented on the stage for a gender critique to take place or for a feminist politic to underlie the dramaturgy'.[39] Systems of patriarchal control in which women have no place is, therefore, as Reinelt proposes, highly relevant to feminist concerns. The absence of women in the realm of the symbolic points to the patriarchal control and 'softcop' policing of social, political, cultural and theatrical sign-systems.

In brief, this shows how hard it is to separate Churchill's politics from her feminism. One might easily, for example refigure the discussion of *Owners* through the socialist lens of this chapter, and, similarly, it is impossible not to come back to the feminist impulse which inflects the socialist concerns of the plays studied in this chapter.

4

Communities in
Dramatic Dialogue

Research has always been important to Caryl Churchill's theatre-making. In prefaces, introductions, afterwords and interviews where she discusses her work, Churchill cites sources and publications which have helped to shape her drama, and, in this way, she permits the reader access to the thinking and making process of her work and ideas.[1] Additionally, she also acknowledges her debt to group work, with companies such as Monstrous Regiment and Joint Stock, as detailed in the previous two chapters, and to directors, designers, and so on, who have collaborated with her in the theatrical process.

Research and the sharing of ideas underpin the three plays studied in this chapter in a special kind of way: they are all projects which involved Churchill, and the company she was working with, in oral research with particular communities. The first of these, *Fen* (1983), was researched by Joint Stock out in a remote East Anglian fen village. *Serious Money* (1987) took Churchill and actors from the Royal Court into London's world of high finance, and *Mad Forest* (1990) involved her and students from the Central School of Speech and Drama in a field-trip to Romania to grapple with political upheaval in Eastern Europe. All three projects relied on meeting with and engaging in dialogue with people involved in each community, whether in East Anglia, London, or Bucharest.

'LAND-GIRLS': *FEN*

In 1983, the year of *Fen*'s production, Mary Chamberlain published a revised edition of her collection of interviews,

Fenwomen, which documents the experiences of girlhood, schooling, marriage, work, religion, politics, recreation and ageing of women in a Fen village.[2] Churchill acknowledges her debt to this study (from which she took quotations for the 'Girls' Song' in Scene Seven),[3] but, like Chamberlain, she and Joint Stock, also conducted their own oral research. Through talking to people, the actors learned about the lives, the work, and the history of the Fen community. As Chamberlain explains, researching orally in this way, the representation of 'people's words and memories' are 'not the silent labours of a solitary archivist, but the result of a dialogue'.[4] Moreover, she argues that researching oral history 'offers the possibility of creating a democratic history in that it offers the means of expression for the past of the "common people"and offers a participation in that process'.[5] *Fen* is 'the result of a dialogue' with a community, and, arguably, demonstrates Churchill using theatre to stage 'democratic history', as she did in *Light Shining in Buckinghamshire.*

Churchill has described *Fen* as the 'most documentary' of her Joint Stock projects,[6] noting that '*Fen* is a play with more direct quotes of things people said to us than any other I've written' (P2 ix). During the period of research, the actors would not record or write down what people said to them, but would go back to the company to present a person they had met to the group.[7] Out of this material Churchill devised a cast of twenty-two characters originally shared between a company of six performers. Reviewing the production, Michelene Wandor criticized the researching and workshopping method for the way in which it was 'reflected in the structure of the piece – a large number of characters representing as many different types of people as can be crammed in'.[8] However, like *Light Shining in Buckinghamshire* or *Vinegar Tom,* as a representation of 'democratic history' the emphasis in *Fen* is on the portrait of a collective rather than the individual; on the representation of a community of ordinary, oppressed people.

The community in *Fen* is largely, although not exclusively, represented by different generations of women who are shown working the land and looking after their homes and children. It is portrayed as a never-ending cycle of drudgery and oppression, passed on from generation to generation; from mothers to daughters. The monotony of the work cycle is imaged in Scene

Two, for example, which shows the women working out in a potato field. Churchill's directions state that they work *'in a row... When their buckets are full they tip the potatoes into a potato grave at the top of the field'* (P2 148). The young women in the community may have their aspirations, as Churchill represents in the lyrics of the 'Girls' Song', but ultimately their dreams do not take them beyond the village which binds them to harsh work on the land, early marriages and child-rearing: 'I want to be a nurse when I grow up/ And I want to have children and get married./ But I don't think I'll leave the village when I grow up' (P2 157). The future for them, as for Angie in *Top Girls*, is 'frightening'. It is through the theatricalization of the ordinary lives of the Fenwomen that the documentary style which Churchill argues for *Fen* is clearly illustrated. Compare Churchill's dramatic documentation, for example, with this brief extract from a factual account of 'Everyday Life of the Fen':

> One of the factors is inherent to the fens and it is an attitude of fear; 'better not step out of line or the employer will have me out'. This is obviously the result of many years hard work and exploitation. Also the fens are very much closed village communities with little opportunity for employment. Even if the girl does receive a decent education and is encouraged to take it seriously there will be very limited job opportunities at the end of it. Therefore the only way to get a good job is to move out of the area and again the fen attitude tends to want not to leave their home village and family.[9]

The cycle of oppression is reinforced in *Fen* by the central figure of Val, who attempts but fails to resist her social destiny. She tries to escape to London with her two daughters and her lover, Frank, but stays tied to the village, recognizing that they do not have the work skills to survive in the city. In order to be with Frank, Val has to give up her daughters. Scene Four, which shows her leaving the children, undercuts the transitory moment of happiness in a wordless Scene Five, in which Val and Frank are seen dancing together: *'Old-fashioned, formal, romantic, happy'* (P2 153). Romance was not something which, as Mary Chamberlain's research revealed, Fenwomen experienced as part of their lives:

> Romance and glamour – the opium of women – had, they felt, passed the fen by. For life on the land is neither romantic nor glamorous. Just hard work, in uncompromising weather, in rough

old working clothes padded out with newspaper against the wind. Small chance to catch a young man's fancy. Marriage for convenience or marriage to conform, particularly for the older women. Then back to the soil. Land worker, home servicer.[10]

When Val is shunned by her community for leaving her children in pursuit of romance and happiness, she takes refuge in religion, which turns out to be a farcical sham of sisterly bonding and comfort, and, ultimately, finding that she can neither live with Frank without her children, nor be with her children without Frank, she invites her lover to kill her as the only means of escaping.

Each time Val turns to women in her family or in her community of friends for help, they preach acceptance rather than resistance. As Shirley, a field-worker and fifty-year-old grandmother counsels, 'You've too much time on your hands. You start thinking. Can't think when you're working in the field can you?' (P2 168). Women like Val, who want to change the oppressive patterning of their lives are seen as deviant, are represented as misfits by their community. Nell, for example, who is one of the few women to protest her rights as a worker (P2 150, 180), is taunted by the village girls for her 'morphrodite' body (P2 155), and Shirley's rebellious granddaughter Sukey is singled out for comment because of her green hair. Val argues, 'Sukey's a freak round here but if she went to a city she wouldn't be, not so much', adding, 'And I wouldn't' (P2 168).

Val, who doubles with the ghost of a nineteenth-century mother and farm-worker whose 'baby died starving' (P2 163), and the generations of women dramatized alongside her, represent the silenced history of the Fenwomen. As one reviewer explained, 'the mothers, daughters and granddaughters whose voices the play amplifies serve as a Greek chorus for a hitherto silent pageant of female emotion'.[11] The focus on the women as representative of the Fen community is significant because it is the women who are doubly oppressed, by their class and by their gender. The ties that bind them to the village, as Val discovers, are financial as well as familial. The double oppression of work and domesticity was visually represented in the set for the original production, for which designer Annie Smart created a field as the 'floor' to both exterior and interior scenes. The presence of the flat, bleak, landscape of the fens further served as a visual counterpoint to the linguistic register of dreams, romance, and story-telling which the women use as a means of 'escape', illustrated, for example, in Angela's dream of living in the 'romantic' rural landscape of the Lake District (*P2* 181), or Nell's diversionary tale of passion and murder (which prefigures Val's 'murder'), narrated while the women pack onions into boxes (Scene Ten).

Class and gender oppression are also encoded in the ensemble style of playing which Churchill's text invites. The one male performer in the original Joint Stock production, who was assigned four character roles, had to play both the oppressed farm-worker and the landowning farmer, thereby marking the discourse of oppressor and oppressed on and through his body. This is highlighted in Scene Three when the actor playing Frank mimes working on a tractor as he carries on a dialogue with Tewson, the farmer: Frank argues in favour of higher wages, while the farmer argues against him. The split-subject dialogue is visually underlined in the gestural encoding of oppressor and oppressed as Frank hits Tewson, that is, '*he hits himself across the face*' (*P2* 151). Similarly, Scene Six stages an oppressor and oppressed relationship between a stepmother, Angela, and her stepdaughter, Becky. The violent nature of their relationship is gesturally represented by Angela forcing Becky to drink a cup of very hot water, while Angela taunts Becky about her absent, dead mother. The absence of the real mother, who signifies comfort and security, and the reality of the stepmother, who represents violence and danger, are gesturally marked in the dual movement from 'good' to 'bad' mother at the close of the scene, as '*Angela strokes Becky's hair then yanks it*' (*P2* 154).

A feel for the violence in the Fen community, and a history of violence in the Fens, such as the nineteenth-century food riots, came out of the oral research. Churchill noted that discontent in the community was the kind that turned itself into aimless violence, rather than being channelled in a political direction.[12] *Fen* illustrates the little impact which the political activities of the union, past and present, have had in improving the lives of ordinary workers. The recollections of Fenwoman Ivy on her ninetieth birthday narrate the generations of landowners in the Tewson family who intimidated the workers to try and prevent them joining the unions:

Fellow come round on his bike and made his speech in the empty street and everybody'd be in the house listening because they daren't go out because what old Tewson might say. 'Vote for the blues, boys,' he'd say and he'd give them money to drink. They'd pull off the blue ribbons behind the hedge. Still have the drink though. (P2 177–8)

In the present, scenes of the women working the fields for a nineteenth-century style of gangmaster, empowered to hire, fire and set the level of wages, demonstrate their exploitation and lack of job security or employment rights (Scenes Two and Twelve). By making the gangmaster a woman, Churchill demonstrates, as she does in *Top Girls*, that it is not just men who abuse women from a position of power. Exploitation is further underlined by the juxtaposition of, for example, Scene Two with Scene One which opens with a Japanese Businessman assigned a monologue detailing the history of capitalist investors in the fens. In the present, landowners like Tewson, selling out to city investors because of taxes on the land (see Scene Nine), perpetuate the history of the capitalist cycle of exploiters and exploited.

Val's 'murder' at the close of the play marks a shift in register from sparse realism to a surreal discourse which links past and present suffering in a resistant vision of fen misery. Angela, who inflicts pain on Becky to anaesthetise her own misery is made to feel her own pain. Nell is seen striding out on stilts like her ancestors who rebelled against the draining of the Fens. Shirley, whose class and gender oppression is imaged in the sight of her ironing the field, remembers what it feels like to be unhappy. The boy from the last century who scares the crows crosses the landscape. Finally, Val's mother May, who would never sing because she could never fulfil her dream of becoming a singer, sings. This is not a utopian realization of her dream, but a recognition of missed opportunity, signalled in the closing Brechtian *Gestus* of May *'stand[ing] as if singing'*, as the spectator hears *'what she would have liked to sing'*, in the form, as Churchill notes for the original production, of *'a short piece of opera on tape'* (P2 145) The dislocation between the voice of the singer and the recorded song signifies the gap between harsh social reality and beautiful dream.

'MONEYSPEAK': *SERIOUS MONEY*

While *Fen* focused on the rural working-class community in East Anglia, *Serious Money* looked at the rise of working-class money-makers in London's changing world of high finance. To research the project, Churchill, Max Stafford-Clark and performers from the Court 'made daily observational forays to the trading floors and dealing rooms of the City', and, as with *Fen*, the performers 'then re-enacted their experiences...in an attempt to create a "work-study" of a community'.[13] This introduced them to the changing practices of the Stock Exchange, engaged them in dialogue with the new 'barrow boy' traders, and taught them the new language of 'serious moneyspeak', 'the current City slang'.[14] As actress Linda Bassett commented, they met people, most of whom seemed to be aged about 23, who were earning between £40,000 and £50,000, when the performers were, at that time, working for a wage of about £130 a week.[15] After the workshopping in the autumn of 1986, Churchill took the research away, spent several months engrossed in the *Financial Times*, before rehearsals and, finally, in March 1987, the production of her 'City comedy' took place. Unlike *Fen's* sympathetic portrait of an oppressed community, *Serious Money* emerged as a satirical critique of the greed and corruption driving the London money markets, and, by implication and association, the Conservative government.

Serious Money is a complex and amoral web of wheeling and (insider) dealing, where the money-makers sacrifice relatives, family, friends, and relationships to make a profit. The dramatic narrative is woven out of two criss-crossing threads: the death (murder?) of commercial paper dealer Jake Todd, and the bid by Billy Corman to take over the company Albion Products. Solving the enigma of Jake's death is the task of his sister Scilla, a LIFFE (London International Financial Futures Exchange) dealer, but she quickly becomes more interested in finding out about how Jake was making enormous sums of 'serious money', and, most importantly, where his money is being held, so that she can claim it for herself. Ultimately the precise cause of Jake's death remains unsolved – although the involvement of the British government, MI5, or the CIA, is hinted at (*P2* 305).

Scilla's investigative drive connects the Albion bid to Jake as she retraces his life through his diary, which contains not events (there's no time for socializing unless business combines with pleasure), but commercial contacts. Through the banker Zackerman (Zac), who supports Corman's bid for Albion, she gets to Corman, and, finally, to the American arbitrageur (a money market speculator), MaryLou Baines. It is Jake's trading in information, enabling speculators like Baines to make their money, which has aroused the suspicions of the DTI – helped by a 'phonecall from an embittered, old-fashioned stock exchange dealer, who is disillusioned with current trading 'standards'. The DTI investigation is, possibly, connected in some way with Jake's death, which, in turn, makes the transatlantic money markets reverberate with fear. As Zac describes, Jake is 'the kind of loose thread' that could make 'the whole fucking city …unravel' (P2 256). (The same kind of fears arose in the 1990s when Nick Leeson's trading bankrupted Barings Bank and made the international money markets nervous.)

The action is condensed into the immediate aftermath of Jake's death, but mixing past and present is realized through flashback sequences, held together by Zac who functions as a narrative linking-device. Theatrically this demonstrates the corrupt money-making practices before and after the Big Bang deregulation of the Stock Exchange. As one critic described it, 'we are in a predatory world where the clubby corruption of the old City is being replaced by the wolfish greed of the deregulated Eighties'.[16] Moreover, Churchill opens her play with a scene from Thomas Shadwell's *The Volunteers, or The Stock-Jobbers*. The imaging of late-seventeenth-century trading among the mercantile classes, seeking to 'turn the penny in the way of stockjobbing' (P2 196), provides a historical example which underscores Churchill's critique of capitalism. As Janelle Reinelt summarizes 'the play's foundation, then, is the Brechtian historicization of finance'.[17]

Scilla and Jake are central not only to the dramatic organization of *Serious Money*, where Jake functions as an enigma and Scilla as investigator, but also to the play's class confrontation between the old boy network and the emergence of the 'barrow boys' in the money markets. Brother and sister are marked by the discourses of both classes: by their property-owning, middle-to-upper-class family, and the class of 'new market makers'. Jake is described by

71

the uneducated dealer Grimes, who has one CSE in metalwork (*P2* 207), as 'the only public schoolboy what can really deal', which Jake claims is 'because I didn't go to university and learn to think twice' (*P2* 205).

As a woman, Scilla has twice offended her familial class: firstly, by going out to work, and, secondly, by going to work without 'being part of an old boy network' (*P2* 281). The warring class discourses are gesturally encoded in Scilla's dialogue precisely because she is a woman engaging in masculine power- and language-play. When, for example, Scilla insists that Zac call MaryLou Baines, so that she can finally make contact with the American speculator with a view to getting her hands on her brother's money, his surprise that she is not the 'English rose' he thought she was, is met with, 'go stick the thorns up your nose, bozo' (*P2* 295–6). And, when Scilla finally meets with MaryLou, she describes herself as a ruthless combination of having the 'cunning and connections of the middle class', while being as 'tough as a yob' (*P2* 305). As the LIFFE scenes at the close of Act One illustrate, women like Scilla who join the money-makers work in a sexist profession, and surviving means speaking the same language. The women use the same 'yob' language about the men as the men do about the women:

JOANNE: Do you call him Dick because he's got spots?
JILL: No, I call him Spot because he's a dick'.

(*P2* 24)

The power-play between the 'old boys' and the new 'barrow boys' is linguistically marked throughout the play. When, for example, the chairman of Albion (England) is under threat from Corman's take-over bid, the 'white knight' (someone who comes to the rescue of a company facing a hostile take-over bid) constructs an image of the company as a 'good old English firm'. In an Arthurian discourse of knights rescuing maidens from villains, Albion (England) is positioned as the maiden and potential rape victim of the villain, Corman (*P2* 235). (The artifice of this strategy is, however, immediately exposed by the white knight's switch from Arthurian imagery to his pragmatic 'we can talk about closing Scunthorpe later', *P2* 235.)

Corman also represents the take-over bid as a sexual act, but not in Arthurian terms, rather as a rapacious act of 'screwing'.

'Sexy greedy *is* the late eighties', argues the PR consultant trying to construct an image for Corman in his fight for Albion (*P2* 287). Screw others before they screw you is the ethos of the deregulated 1980s, and 'moneyspeak' is a language trading in sexual obscenities. To make money is, as Ian Dury's lyrics to the song which brings Act One to a close state, to 'do the fucking business' (*P2* 253). Moreover, 'Do[ing] the fucking business' leaves no time for the 'business of fucking', as comically illustrated in the inability of Zac and Jacinta Condor (a Peruvian business woman) in the second act, to find a 'window' for pleasure (sex).

Traders no longer buy and sell products, but deal in one commodity: money. As Scilla explains in a direct address to the audience: 'You can buy and sell money, you can buy and sell absence of/ money, debt, which used to strike me as funny' (*P2* 244). For economically deprived countries, the act of trading or speaking money is also an act of colonization as Western money markets profit at the expense of the Third World economy. Churchill demonstrates this in the representation of Jacinta, who is both colonized and colonizer. Coming from Peru, she belongs to a country of the oppressed, but money empowers her to colonize by trading in and with the West at the expense of her own nation. As her accomplice, Nigel Abjibala, states: 'One thing one learned from one's colonial masters,/ One makes money from other people's disasters' (*P2* 261). When researching the City, Churchill described how 'one of the actors ... from St. Kitts, was astonished to see that the price of sugar, so important to his country's economy, was determined by what happened in a small room between a few listless young men'. She added, 'that was one of the moments when we could connect what we saw in the City with the world outside'.[18]

Moreover, the colonizing impulse may be read as underpinning the ethos of the corrupt international money markets. Churchill resists any suggestion that the displaced old boys network was somehow morally better than the thoroughly amoral class of new marketeers. All of the characters in her dramatization of the world of high finance are dissolute and espouse the creed of 'do others before they can do you' (*P2* 305). It is the spectator who is positioned as the only potentially moral agent in the performance frame; who is invited through the Brechtian mode of address to cast a critical eye over the world of high finance.

However, reviewers noted that 'despite her [Churchill's] stern intentions, she makes the buccaneering atmosphere of the City seem rather attractive'.[19] Peter Lewis, commenting on the audiences at the Royal Court production, observed that 'at least two City firms booked the entire theatre to take their staff on a kind of Yuppie works outing'.[20] After the transfer to Wyndham's, Jeremy Kingston noted that 'the show's popularity among exactly the people it set out to condemn is one of its more intriguing features', adding that it was 'rather as though coachloads of Venetian Jews had driven up to applaud Mr Shakespeare's play about a vengeful Jewish usurer'.[21] Reported comments from City spectators seemed to indicate that they found it 'very true to life'.[22] In short, the verve of Churchill's writing combined with the high-energy mode of Joint Stock's physical performance style of ensemble playing enabled the spectator to experience the adrenalin, but not always, it would appear, her satirical view of the money market.

Drama scholar Ruby Cohn, while praising the 'demonic energy' of *Serious Money*, blames this failing on Churchill's use of verse, arguing that she finds the play 'hard ... to take seriously as satire', because 'the energetic rhymes pound home the repetitive quality of corruption, unredeemed by any direct or honest statement'.[23] However, this overlooks the way in which Churchill's satirical purpose is clearly signalled in her verse, which she creates out of City slang and obscene 'moneyspeak', alien to the non-City spectator. The programme for the Wyndham's production, for example, included explanations of City scandals and glossaries of the City slang. While those inside the markets may easily read the signs encoded in the different coloured blazers (uniforms) of the traders and understand the language of 'moneyspeak', the non-City spectator is alienated by visual and linguistic sign-systems; is positioned as 'outsider', as critical observer.

Rather, audience reactions to *Serious Money* demonstrate that the dramatist – like the semiotician Pierre in *Softcops* – cannot 'fix' meaning or determine audience response. It further references the complex role of the spectator in the reception process; the spectator as active and acting participant in the production of meaning. If the spectator shares in the ethos of greed and corruption encoded in the performance text, she/he may engage in the pleasure of identification, refusing to 'see' the signs which position her or him as the satirical subject. For example, Ian Dury's second song which closes the play, 'Five More Glorious Years', critiques the 1987 Conservative re-election, heralding a possible further five years of greed and corruption. But the critique may not be 'heard' by those for whom Thatcher's re-election was a cause for celebration; who delighted in the prospect of being 'pissed and promiscuous', earning 'ridiculous' money for another five years (P2 308). Ironically, however, if Churchill's socialist critique was over-turned in one way, it was served in another: the pleasuring of right-wing City audiences helped to make 'serious money' for left-wing theatre.[24]

'TWO WEDDINGS AND A REVOLUTION': *MAD FOREST*

Political systems of power and oppression constitute a dominant motif in *Mad Forest*, Churchill's dramatization of the 1989 Romanian revolution. Having worked with Churchill for Joint Stock, the then artistic director of Central, Mark Wing-Davey, proposed a Joint Stock Style of workshopping for this East European project. This resulted in taking British drama students out to Bucharest to stay with the families of Romanian students with whom they worked and researched. Again, much of the research for *Mad Forest* was conducted out on the street, talking to ordinary Romanian people.[25] For Churchill, taking students out to Romania to research this project was a way of 'working away from the mainstream' with young people who were 'the same age as the people who made the revolution'.[26]

The research trip to Romania took place just a few months after the fall of Ceausescu in December 1989, and therefore at a moment of post-revolutionary chaos as Romanian citizens were trying to take stock of what had happened and what the future held for them. While Churchill worked on *Mad Forest* for its production in June 1990, Romania was struggling to come to terms with the election of Illiescu and the National Salvation Front, associated with the old Ceausescu regime, and, as the play opened, students were again being subjected to violence as miners in Bucharest were brought in to crush anti-Front protesters. Some reviewers were critical of Mad Forest for failing to tackle this latest twist in events, although it is difficult to see how theatre can keep pace with the real life drama of events. Reviewer Benedict Nightingale offered a practical piece of advice: 'Churchill should keep Mad Forest in her word-processor, ready to up-date, revise. It could become one of her most striking plays'.[27]

Nightingale also had praise for the way in which the 'unfinished feel' of Mad Forest succeeded in capturing the real-life chaos of revolution and history in the making. The 'unfinished feel' is created through the dramatization of fragments from the lives of ordinary people – orally researched by the cast – from before, during and after the revolution. Two weddings frame this three-part structure, situated either side of the second, middle section which represents the revolution of December 1989. The first and third sections trace the lives of two families, one working class (the Vladu family) and one middle class (the Antonescu family), and the ways in which their lives are conditioned by the oppressive Ceausescu regime and post-liberation disorder. The Vladu family are especially affected in the opening section by the marriage of their daughter Lucia, to an American – a 'betrayal' which places the whole family under the surveillance of the secret police. Further tensions arise from this wedding, which concludes the first section, as it makes it difficult for the cross-class marriage between Lucia's sister Florina, and Radu, from the Antonescu family, to take place. The revolution is what makes the second wedding possible.

Where Serious Money uses the City language of 'moneyspeak' to drive the action on, Mad Forest shows people afraid to communicate, to act through speaking In Part One, revolution can only be whispered in meat-buying queues (MF 17), or joked about in low voices among trusted friends (MF 20–21). As people are afraid of how their own words might be used against them, familial conversation is either silenced or conducted only when the radio is turned up loud (MF 13). Bogdan's protest over the prospect of his daughter marrying an American is enacted visually rather than verbally: he smashes one of four eggs which Lucia offers to her family with her American cigarettes (MF 13).

(The egg is quickly salvaged by Bogdan's wife, Irina. It is too precious to waste.) Public speech is reserved for the praise of Ceausescu, as illustrated in the teacher, Flavia Antonescu, addressing her pupils in a monologue on the merits of the president (*MF* 16). Privately, however, a dialogue between Flavia and her dead grandmother, reveals the numbness she feels at living a lie; living a life that 'nobody's living' (*MF* 26). That Flavia's thoughts and feelings are shared with a figure who is already dead underlines the risks of speaking openly with the living. Similarly, a priest, seeking comfort from the danger of talking, holds a conversation with an Angel:

> This is so sweet, like looking at the colour blue, like looking at the sky when you're a child lying on your back, you stare out at the blue but you're going in, further and further in away from the world, that's what it's like knowing I can talk to you. Someone says something, you say something back, you're called to a police station, that happened to my brother. So it's not safe to go out to people and when you can't go out sometimes you find you can't go in, I'm afraid to go inside myself, perhaps there's nothing there, I just keep still. But I can talk to you, no one's ever known an angel work for the Securitate. (*MF* 21)

The gap or contradiction between what is said and what is unspoken is demonstrated in a scene in which Lucia asks a doctor for an abortion. The dialogue involves Lucia making her request and the doctor refusing her request, but, at the same time, they carry on a silent exchange of words (on paper) during which the abortion is agreed to and paid for:

> DOCTOR: There is no abortion in Romania. I am shocked that you even think of it. I am appalled that you dare suggest I might commit this crime.
> LUCIA: Yes, I'm sorry.
> *LUCIA gives the doctor an envelope thick with money and some more money.*
> DOCTOR: Can you get married?
> LUCIA: Yes.
> DOCTOR: Good. Get married.
> *The DOCTOR writes again, LUCIA nods.*
> DOCTOR: I can do nothing for you. Goodbye.
> *Lucia smiles. She makes her face serious again.*
> LUCIA: Goodbye.
>
> (*MF* 19)

As Janelle Reinelt explains, 'these different Brechtian gests of talking (or not) enable the relationship between communication and ideology to become visible'.[28]

The Brechtian style of *Mad Forest* is structurally encoded in the three-part montage of scenes, captioned with titles announced in Romanian and English. As Churchill instructs that a performer reads these titles in the manner of an English tourist using a Romanian phrase book (*MF* 13), the difficulty of expression is again underlined. In Part Two, one is forcefully reminded of Brecht's revolutionary street scene in *The Mother*. Here, using a technique which recalls the multiple role-switching in *Light Shining in Buckinghamshire*, which Churchill used to portray the chaos of a (potentially) revolutionary moment, the performers break with their character roles from Part One to represent different Romanian citizens caught up in the December upheaval from 'order' to 'unorder'. The performers were instructed for this section to play their parts in the manner of Romanians speaking with English accents. This technique gave 'a startlingly vivid sense of real events being recalled in the immediate aftermath'.[29] In contrast to Part One, where language has lost its performative function, in Part Two, the revolution is performed through speaking. This was underlined by keeping the performers physically still on stage, posed 'as if for a group photograph', rather than using the revolutionary section of the play as 'an obvious chance for characters to rush around the stage waving flags with holes cut out of them'.[30]

A surreal scene between a vampire and a dog opens the third part, imaging Romania as the poor, starving, ownerless, dog, missing the hated master and looking to the Vampire as a new blood-sucking owner. As the revolution releases the Romanian citizens into speech, confusion and tensions begin to surface. Parents and children are divided over support of new political parties, specifically over whether to be pro- or anti-Front, and racism towards the Hungarians is a source of heated familial debate. Where Lucia created tension in Part One through her marriage to an American, she causes upset in Part Three through the renewal of her relationship with a Hungarian lover. New political 'freedoms' bring new oppressions as citizens like Flavia, who kept their jobs under the old regime, now find their positions at risk. In the hospital where Gabriel Vladu, treated as a wounded hero of the revolution, recuperates, a disorientated patient, representative of post-revolution confusion, wanders the wards asking what had really happened: 'Did we have a revolution or a putsch?' (*MF* 50) – a line which was greeted with applause when the play was performed in Bucharest.[31]

The re-enactment of the revolution is a theatrical device which Churchill uses in Part Three to dramatize the questions and uncertainties which the Romanians need to express. The wedding couple, Florina and Radu, role-play the execution of the Ceausescus, a sequence which releases hatred, sexism and racism (*MF* 68–71). The wedding, which Flavia compares to the revolution where 'everyone laughs and cries' and goes 'back behind their masks' (*MF* 74), re-enacts the before, during and after moments of the revolution, as the polite, public 'masks' are shattered by outbreaks of verbal and physical violence, followed by a silent dance – a ritualized moment of enforced social harmony, which gives way to a renewed linguistic outbreak (in Romanian) of political and social discontents. Churchill uses the high-energy technique of overlapping voices, as she did in *Serious Money*, to demonstrate the passionate and violent release into 'freedom' which the revolution brings. She assigns the final lines of *Mad Forest* to the figure of the blood-sucking Vampire who haunts the wedding dance, and instructs that his last few words should be heard alone: 'You begin to want blood. Your limbs ache, your head burns, you have to keep moving faster and faster' (*MF* 87).

Post-revolutionary 'freedom' offers new possibilities, but like the post-murder release of pain and suffering in *Fen*, or the post-election chorus of 'five fucking morious' years of Tory corruption in *Serious Money*, the future for the Romanian people, trying to find their way through the 'Mad (political) Forest' is also 'frightening'.

5

Exploding Words
and Worlds

'Playwrights don't give answers, they ask questions', wrote
Churchill in an early essay on theatre.[1] She continued: 'We need
to find new questions, which may help us answer the old ones
or make them unimportant, and this means new subjects and
new form'.[2] The kinds of questions which Churchill asks
through her theatre reflect her feminist and socialist view-
points, but allied to her interrogative, political mode of writing
is her experimental approach to dramatic and theatrical form.
Churchill's theatre is not just a question of politics, but a politics
of style.

This final chapter seeks to highlight Churchill's experimental
approach to theatre-making by examining her interest in the
defamiliarization of our twentieth-century fictions or systems of
illusion-making, which she encodes thematically (subject) and
stylistically (form) in a range of plays. In particular, it examines
Churchill's deformation or explosion of the word, of language,
the sign-system through which we mediate and make sense of
the world, whether this is in the context of postmodern culture,
as in her late 1980s play *Icecream*, or the mythological
underworld of one of her most recent, iconoclastic productions, *The Skriker* (1994).

By way of introduction, I wish to return briefly to an earlier
period of Churchill's work: specifically to *Traps*, written in 1976
along with *Vinegar Tom* and *Light Shining in Buckinghamshire*,
which shows Churchill's early preoccupation with manipulat-
ing sign-systems; with 'unfixing' the boundaries of illusion and
reality. In the uncertain, unstable, and violent dramatic world of
Traps, Churchill violates the illusion- and reality-making rules to

create a 'reality' that has no existence other than on the stage, like 'an impossible object, or a painting by Escher, where the objects can exist like that on paper, but would be impossible in life' (*P1* 71). The dramatic world of *Traps* operates through sign-systems which are constantly destabilized: a group of six characters gather in a room which is urbanly and then rurally located; a door which opens for one character appears locked for another; clothes which we see being ironed are re-presented in a crumpled state for ironing; a bowl and plant, which get broken and destroyed, reappear as new; a woman with a baby speaks of not having a baby, and a man talked about as dead walks into the room alive. The dramatic universe is like a Mobius strip, 'the loop [which] has only one surface' (*P1* 71). In a world in which 'it would be nice to have a family' (*P1* 92), where it would be possible to 'walk down a normal street...or eat dinner in a normal restaurant' (*P1* 79), nothing is 'normal'. Everything is made strange.

As an ideological and formal experiment with the artifice of the 'real', Churchill baffled critics, who complained that the play's 'purpose...remains obscure'.[3] Those like Irving Wardle, who insisted on trying to describe the drama in traditional terms of what happens and who is who, eventually had to admit (disgruntled) defeat.[4] In challenging the ways in which we make sense of meaning, Churchill's experimental style demanded a different 'reading' of the staged world: one where rules are broken and meaning is constantly being made and unmade through the language of performance rather than the word of the dramatic script. This is a characteristic of all the plays discussed in this final chapter, beginning with Churchill's 1986 production, *A Mouthful of Birds*.

'UNDEFENDED DAYS': *A MOUTHFUL OF BIRDS*

'I wanted to get away from words', was an explanation which Churchill offered to one reviewer for her production of *A Mouthful of Birds*, co-written with David Lan.[5] In order 'to get away from words' Churchill extended the processes of collaboration to include not just a co-writer, but also a choreographer, namely Ian Spink, director of Second Stride dance company. Churchill had hoped that Spink would work with her on *Fen*, but this had not been possible (*LGP* viii). She had the opportunity to be involved as a writer in a collaborative performance art piece after *Fen*, *Midday Sun* (1984),[6] but was not able to work with Spink until the 1986 production. Where Churchill and Lan shared in the writing process, Spink and Les Waters (director of *Fen*) shared the direction. The play was again workshopped by members of the Joint Stock company, although, unusually in this instance, the group worked intensively and continuously for a twelve-week period without the customary 'writing gap'.[7]

A Mouthful of Birds is fashioned out of seven stories of possession which take their cue from Euripides's *The Bacchae*. As Churchill explains, they did not set out to 'do a version of *The Bacchae* but to look at the same issues of possession, violence and ecstasy' (*MB* 5). The play opens with snapshots from the lives of seven characters: Lena a mother, Marcia a switchboard operator, Derek an unemployed person, Yvonne an acupuncturist, Paul a businessman, Dan a vicar, and Doreen a secretary. The seven characters then excuse themselves from their everyday habits, routines, and commitments and give themselves up to 'an "undefended day" in which there is nothing to protect you from the forces inside and outside yourself' (*MB* 5). Each character goes through her or his own extreme possession sequence. These sequences make up the second, middle part of the play. In a final, third part each character talks, monologue style, about the changes in their lives as a consequence of experiencing possession. As one character summarizes, living through the extremes, experiencing the pleasure of violence, is the 'power' she 'like[s] best in the world. The struggle is every day not to use it' (*MB* 70). Or, as Churchill herself explained,

> For a lot of people, as well as it [violence] being horrible, there is a sort of pleasure in things being so terrible and so extreme. You have to recognise it, otherwise you're only trying to resist it on a rational level which just says this is bad and we don't want it. Actually it's not as simple as that. It's a thing of using your strength and power.[8]

Where Lan's anthropological interest in possession connected to his research of the 'spirit world' in Zimbabwe, used to fight against the oppression of the Smith regime,[9] one of Churchill's 'starting points' was her interest in women and violence (*MB* 5). She was attracted to the demythologization of gender stereotyping which encodes women as peaceful, men as violent. At the start of the play, the women tend to conform to traditional stereotypes; they occupy servicing roles, administering to the needs of others. In possession sequences, however, women demonstrate a capacity for violence which violates 'naturalized' images of femininity. The mother, Lena, for example, is possessed by a spirit who urges her to commit infanticide. A breakfast-time scenario is acted out on four successive days during which Lena is subjected to the split voices of her husband chattering about inconsequentialities (a role stereotypically assigned to women), and of the spirit ordering her to kill the baby. The consequence of this dual logocentric attack on Lena is the killing of the baby, imaged in the washing of a shawl in a baby bath (*MB* 27). Lena states quite simply 'it wasn't me that did it' (*MB* 28).

The secretary Doreen's possession sequence, 'Hot Summer', images another taboo: women being violent with women. The sequence, which begins with a woman-centred text – Doreen speaks of her aching body while it is massaged by another woman – changes register as a woman called Lil verbalizes narratives of violence from a newspaper, to a score of domestic sounds created as Doreen and another woman, Mrs Blair, 'wound' (drown) each other in sound: turning up radios, banging saucepans, knocking over chairs and smashing cutlery. This climaxes in a ritualization of physical violence: Doreen slashes Mrs Blair's face, rolls her body up in a carpet, rolls her out, and the scene resumes quietly, still punctuated by the reading of narratives of violence. Like Lena, Doreen has a one-line explanation, 'all I wanted was peace and quiet' (*MB* 58), delivered directly to the audience at the start of the sequence.

In both of these possession sequences women are aurally assaulted, which initiates a violent release of energy in which they are seen to harm themselves, each other, and, in Lena's case, a daughter. In the final part of Doreen's sequence, she and other women turn their energies from the inward movement of hurting themselves (imaged, for example, in Doreen biting her arm), to an outwards movement, concentrating them into the power to move objects which they send *'flying across the room'*

(*MB* 66). In the bounded world of the 'rational', women are not able to experience the power of flight.[10] In 'carry[ing]' on her role as secretary, which Doreen describes at the end of the play, she has to repress the memory of violence and of flying; extreme experiences collapsed in the imaging of a 'mouth ... full of birds which I crunch between my teeth. Their feathers, their blood and broken bones are choking me' (*MB* 71).[11]

The other woman-centred possession sequences are that of Marcia, who as a black medium is colonized by a white spirit, and Yvonne, who struggles with an altogether different spirit in the shape of alcohol. However, critiquing gender stereotypes is not restricted to femininity, but also extends to masculinity. Paul's business discourse – the successful capitalist trading in meat – is displaced in his sequence by a discourse marked by the romantic (traditionally assigned to women), as he falls in love with a pig. Dan, the vicar, announces to the audience at the start of his sequence: 'I don't believe god is necessarily male' (*MB* 37). As he dances, his female and male 'victims' die of pleasure. The dance register encoding androgyny, death and ecstasy is played out against a dialogue shared between a male and female prison officer who attempt, linguistically, to 'fix' the ambiguously gendered body of a multiple murderer.

The 'unfixing' of gendered bodies is most clearly marked in Derek's story, which occupies a central position in the play, opening the second act. In the first act, Derek is introduced as a man who compensates for the emasculation of unemployment through weight training, which marks the body in the sphere of the masculine. He states that he will not be like his father who 'thought he wasn't a man without a job' and 'died within six weeks' (*MB* 20). However, in his possession sequence, played in the presence of Dionysos, he is 'seduced' by the figure of Herculine Barbin. Herculine Barbin/e was a nineteenth-century hermaphrodite who began life as a 'woman', was brought up in a convent, was later redefined as a 'man', and, as a result, committed suicide. Foucault's introduction to the diary memoirs *Herculine Barbin* opens with the question, 'Do we *truly* need a *true* sex?'[12] As Foucault's introduction makes clear, it is the insistence of Western society on a 'true sex' which has gendered the body 'in an order of things where one might have imagined that all that counted was the reality of the body and the intensity of its pleasures'.[13] Derek's possession sequence questions the binary ordering of gender, as Herculine Barbin, played by a woman dressed as a man, verbalizes her/his narrative, while passing *'objects from her past'* to Derek (*MB* 51). Her/his narrative is repeated by Derek who *'holds all the objects and has dressed himself in the shawl and petticoat'* (*MB* 52). As Derek repeats the Herculine narrative, Herculine *'stands beside him and takes the objects from him and packs them into her suitcase'* (*MB* 52). As the final signs of femininity are taken away (shawl and petticoat), Derek repeats the loss of the feminine self: 'Sara's body, my girl's body, all lost' (*MB* 54). Appealing to Herculine, who has the 'feminine' packed away in her/his suitcase, he asks 'couldn't you have stayed?', whereupon she/he *'turns back and kisses him on the neck'* (*MB* 54) – indexing the pleasure of the 'unfixed' hermaphroditic body not as two sexes in one, but two bodies as one sex.

In the re-imaging of the murder from *The Bacchae*, which brings the middle possession sequences of the play to a close, it is Derek who, possessed by Pentheus, is dressed as a woman and is torn to pieces by the women. His final monologue, entitled 'body', speaks of his desire for the feminine. Like Schreber, Derek takes pleasure in the corporeal experience of the feminine and he describes the pleasure in his breasts and his waist which 'isn't small but it makes me smile' (*MB* 71). He has 'almost forgotten the man who possessed this body'. The fixed, gendered body of the masculine, a 'skin [which] used to wrap me up', is now open and in flux – 'it lets the world in' (*MB* 71).

Using the body to explore extremes of violence, passion and ecstasy is also a means of exploding the 'word' which binds us to the symbolic 'order of things' in the world of the rational. Spink's movement-based performance register was, therefore, central to the enactment of the 'undefended days'. The dance register was used to create visual, physical texts between scenes, to punctuate or counterpoint verbal sequences, and to encode the classical Greek text in the modern 'world'. As a performance register it was used to signify the relationship between the performer and character and her or his body: 'When the victims dance it is a jerky, autistic ballet of imprisonment. Only when the two figures of Dionysus . . . take the stage does it expand into the flowing line of those who are at peace with their own bodies'.[14] Working with a physical register enabled transgressive movement between pain and pleasure, terror and ecstasy, life and death, as, for example, in the Fruit Ballet where performers imaged *'the sensuous pleasures of eating and the terrors of being torn up'* (*MB* 28), in Dan's dancing to his victims who died of pleasure, and in the death of Pentheus which used dance to recreate moments of extreme violence and happiness from the play.

As was the case with *Traps*, it is doubtful whether from an audience's and critic's point of view the 'purpose' of *A Mouthful of Birds* was entirely clear. Critics commented repeatedly on spectators walking out before the interval, or, as one reviewer stated, sitting 'it out to the end possessed by a tedium as painfully intense as anything which was happening on stage'.[15] Reviewer Nicholas de Jongh argued that 'this extravaganza of dreamy work, mime and dance does have a clear line of argument and exposition' which was, however, 'easily missed if you do not first read the text'.[16] This suggests that 'getting away from words' posed a difficulty for the British playgoer, educated in a tradition of text-based theatre, but unable to 'read' the physical language of the stage out of which *A Mouthful of Birds* takes its shape.

IDENTITY, CULTURE AND THE POSTMODERN: *ICECREAM*

Churchill's 1989 play *Icecream* also relies on an ability to 'read' the visual, but in a very different way to *A Mouthful of Birds*. For this drama, Churchill returned to working on her own after the workshopping experience of *Serious Money*, which began as *Mouthful of Birds* opened, and further collaboration with Spink in *Fugue*, a dance-drama broadcast on Channel 4 television in 1988.

Like *Traps*, *Icecream* is an exploration and exposition of illusion- and reality-making,[17] but drawing on a more complex and developed counterpointing of visual and verbal 'texts'. There are two acts which are set in Britain and America respectively. As the play opens, an American couple, Lance and Vera, are seen holidaying in Britain. The way in which they 'see' Britain is, however, through tourist images and sign-systems of popular culture. In approaching the Highlands, for example, Lance and Vera sing snatches of half-remembered Scottish ballads, and a refrain from the movie *Brigadoon*. They 'locate' British heritage and culture in a castle setting and a traditional Devon cottage.

By contrast, the quest for heritage takes the American couple out of clichéd tourist locations as they trace Lance's family history to a flat in East London where they find their distant English cousins, Phil and Jaq. This transatlantic encounter occasions a cross-cultural exchange of (mis)-perceived English-ness and Americanicity. If the Americans characterize England as 'the green fields. The accents. The Pubs' (*IC* 11), then the English see America as 'Old Cadillacs. Cactus. Long straight roads' (*IC* 9). Although all four characters speak English, an 'international language' (*IC* 41), it is difference and lack of cultural commonality which emerge, shown, for example, in the different meanings which the same word has in each culture, or how a word like 'icecream' is pronounced differently by English and American speakers.[18]

Loathing for 'American filth' also creeps into Phil's discourse (*IC* 9); a linguistic marker which signals a more sinister note and change in dramatic register. An illicit kiss between Phil and Vera prefigures a violent event, as Phil presents the others with the body of a man he has murdered. As Lance and Vera are drawn into helping dispose of the body in Epping Forest, their English breakfasts no longer delight them, and the idyllic English countryside now represents terror rather than pleasure.

In Act Two, Lance and Vera have returned to America having lent the remainder of their holiday money to Phil, who is convinced that his cousins, like all Americans, have 'plenty of money' (*IC* 24). They are then surprised by Jaq and Phil turning up at their home in America. It is now the turn of the English cousins to play the tourist game as they want to see all the famous sights: 'New York and New Orleans...the Rocky Mountains...the Everglades...the Grand Canyon...Disney-land and Hollywood' (*IC* 32). Again, events take an unexpected turn as Phil is hit by a car (apparently he may have stepped out into the road looking the wrong way),[19] and is killed. Jaq takes to the American roads in Lance and Vera's car on a journey which culminates in a second murder when she (*Thelma and Louise* style) kills an American professor who attempts to assault her. Returning to Lance and Vera, Jaq begs the money for a ticket to

England, although the final scene at the airport shows her tempted to change her 'destination' and to accompany a South American woman on her flight home.

Taking a descriptive line on *Icecream*, as he did with *Traps*, Irving Wardle confessed to not understanding the play 'beyond its assertion that England and America are more dangerous places than tourist brochures suggest'.[20] While *Icecream* is arguably a more obscure piece than some of Churchill's straightforwardly political and/or feminist plays, her interest in what she describes as 'writing more intuitively' in *Icecream* also has a political dimension.[21] As she herself explains, this may not mean 'actually saying "here is a political course of action"', but of 'throwing up worries and questions and complexities which you might not have if you weren't of a particular political complexion'.[22] In *Icecream* the 'worries and questions and complexities' which the play theatricalizes are a reflection on the politics of the postmodern condition, characterized by collapsing cultures, identities, or as Janelle Reinelt and Joseph Roach (via Lyotard) explain, 'the collapse of categories themselves, an implosion that has been attributed to the media-saturated powers of capitalistic production and consumption'.[23] As a 'culture of "hyper-representation"',[24] the postmodern generates anxiety because it is no longer possible to know what is 'real'. In her commentary on advertising in the British media in the late 1980s, Suzanne Moore elaborated on this 'hyper-representation' and question of anxiety, by explaining the postmodern as:

> a time when signs – both visual and linguistic – are no longer monogamous with what they refer to in the 'real' world. They have instead started to copulate madly with each other, producing potential meaning everywhere. In this 'loss of the real', these illegitimate meanings are no longer anchored by the morality of one-to-one representation, float off to produce endless simulations, images of images, fakes of fakes – the past is there to be reinvented because surface reveals not depth, just more surface.[25]

It is this 'loss of the real', the loss of identity and culture in the artifice of the postmodern Western world, which is dramatized in *Icecream*.

Icecream encodes the postmodern interplay of images through its constant referencing of media and cinematic sign-systems, also reflected in Peter Hartwell's cinematographic set designs for the UK and American landscapes. In point of fact, Churchill's feel for the piece, when it first came to her in the mid-1980s, was 'more like an idea for a movie'.[26] Reviewer Michael Billington commented:

> Structurally and thematically I was reminded of the movies: The Man Who Knew Too Much meets Paris, Texas. The first half is exactly like a Hitchcockian movie in which a pair of holidaying Americans turn up in Europe and find themselves in a dizzying whorl of violence. The second half is a truncated road-movie that sees rural America as a disquieting place filled with pockets of eccentricity.[27]

Moreover, Billington argued that Churchill's dramatic organization of quick-changing short scenes required 'the ability of a TV and movie-trained audience to supply missing information for themselves. It is a sharp reminder of how much playwriting is changing in the video age'.[28]

'Loss of the real' is also linguistically encoded in *Icecream*. As language is divorced from reality, it is no longer possible to know what is 'real', what is 'true'. Thinking in clichés provides the only access to cultural identity:

> VERA: When I think of my European ancestors I see this long row of women picking cabbages.
> PHIL: Is that what they did?
> VERA: I've no idea, it's a cliché, I guess I think in clichés all the time. It's depressing but then I think hell, clichés are just what's true, what millions of people have already realised is true.
>
> (*IC* 13)

Moreover, speaking in clichés initiates dangerous realities. Vera's clichéd 'I would die' for you, addressed to Phil, is immediately followed by Phil's presentation of the murdered body. Death as a cliché, as a figure of speech, is displaced by the figure of a dead body.

Fictions and truths are constantly represented as interchangeable and unstable. When Vera, for example, at the start of Act Two tries to tell her American 'shrink' the truth about the murder in England, he, in turn, translates this into a Freudian fiction or fantasy linked to the anxiety of identity (*IC* 27). Lance's confession of the murder to a colleague turns the truth into a fictitious account of a sexual encounter (*IC* 29), and the murder, narrated as a party-piece to a listening guest at Lance and Vera's party, re-presents the event as a glamorous (movie-style) adventure, to which the guest responds: 'You got away with murder. My god. Some adventure. Wow. Is this true? Jee-zus' (*IC* 35).

The 'loss of the real' is further highlighted in the latter part of Act Two which is thematically marked by the (in)significance of death. Churchill herself noted, 'I didn't realise until I'd finished writing it how much there is about death and ways of facing death, and about things which are buried rather than being faced'.[29] Jaq does not mourn for her brother but embarks on her road movie,[30] during which she encounters a hitchhiker and his mother, who each have their own apocalyptic visions of the millennium, a professor whose wife has recently died a meaningless death of cancer, and, finally, the South American woman passenger at the airport whose grandfather has died. The significance of endings or death is, however, refused as a possibility in the endless, chaotic play of the postmodern. In the 'closure' of *Icecream*, Jaq is still in her movie, is still speaking in clichés: 'I want to be at home and have a cup of tea' (*IC* 51). Continuous (dis)placement is the only 'home' left in our postmodern Western world which refuses to anchor cultures and identities in the 'real'. However, Churchill offers Jaq a way out of this by allowing her to change destinations: 'she goes off to a third world country, to South America'.[31]

'...LIES AND VIDEO TAPE': *HOT FUDGE*

As *Icecream* played for a short, although very intense, seventy-five minutes, Churchill was persuaded by Max Stafford-Clark to introduce a companion piece which would provide the performers who had minor roles in *Icecream* with main parts (*S* intro). Although Churchill had reservations about whether *Hot Fudge*, the play she wrote to go with *Icecream*, would in some way 'spoil' it (*S* intro), stylistically and thematically the two pieces work well together. *Hot Fudge* was given performance readings during May 1989 in the Royal Court Theatre Upstairs.

In a clipped dialogic patterning of scenes, similar to *Icecream*, *Hot Fudge* continues the illusion- and reality-making theme. Echoes of *Serious Money* haunt the opening in which a group of characters explain how to commit fraud through building-society accounts, falsifying claims to money which does not exist. This modern way of 'stealing' is contrasted with a nostalgia for old-fashioned robbery. *Hot Fudge* encodes the postmodern in its commodification of culture, news and geography, as the two central characters, Ruby and Colin, fabricate identities for themselves: Ruby as an owner of a travel agency, Colin as an owner of a media monitoring company. Colin's circle of 1980s Yuppie friends all have careers and lives trading in images. Getting on is not about having the 'real thing' but of having a 'great image' (*S* 293). When confronted by his ex-wife in front of Ruby, Colin's self-created image begins to shatter. Rather than an international trader in news stories, it is revealed that Colin is an unemployed person who has had a breakdown and who spends his days in the bedroom, drinking lager, and videoing the news. As Ruby voluntarily unmasks her fictions, Colin realizes that just about everything he knows about her is also a 'lie', which leaves the couple at the end of the play starting to get to know each other; beginning all over again.

'DANGEROUS LIAISONS': *LIVES OF THE GREAT POISONERS*

After the experience of working alone on *Icecream*, Churchill turned again to shared ways of working with *Mad Forest* in 1990 and, in 1991, *Lives of the Great Poisoners*, which was to prove her most complex collaborative venture to date.

While poison was a thematic starting point (*LGP* ix), experimenting with form in a multidisciplinary context was another. In terms of 'getting away from words', *Poisoners* not only incorporated movement and dance, but also used music in the form of *a cappella* singing. The physical language out of which *Poisoners* takes its shape is reflected in the publication of a production dossier of the performance, rather than a script. The dossier includes dramatic text, directions for dance, the musical score, production photographs (including set design), and images projected in the performance. The different 'languages' of the stage were overseen as follows: Churchill – script; Ian Spink – movement; Orlando Gough – music; and Antony McDonald – design. As the composer, Gough, was interested in exploring the 'physicality of music-making' (*LGP* xi); Spink wanted a dance style 'that could appear out of the action' (*LGP* xv), and McDonald was concerned with 'blurring the line between choreography and design' (*LGP* xvii). Each contribution therefore linked to formal experiment and the desire to work in a performance register which moved away from traditional text-based theatre.

Whereas in *A Mouthful of Birds* it was the case that all performers, irrespective of whether they were trained dancers rather than actors or actresses, or *vice versa*, had to take part in movement-based and dialogue-based sequences, for *Poisoners* it was decided that performers should work exclusively in their specialist disciplines. Only one exception obtained as an actor doubled as a singer. The other eight performers consisted of four dancers, three singers and one actor (*LGP* xvi). This initiated a mode of interdisciplinary dialogic exchange in which, for example, one character might speak in dialogue to another answering in music or dance, and so on.

Poisoners is composed in three sections, each based on the life of a 'great poisoner': Dr Crippen, Medea and Mme de Brinvilliers. In addition, a prologue entitled 'Elixir of Life' theatricalizes a less well known incident from Medea mythology in which Medea uses poison not to kill but to cure, as she administers a revitalizing potion to Jason's ailing father Aeson (*LGP* 5). Like Marlene in *Top Girls*, Midgley, the one twentieth-century character, is able to pass through all scenes, irrespective of dramatic conventions of time. Midgley is based on the early twentieth-century American chemist Thomas Midgley, who was responsible for putting CFCs in fridges and lead in petrol, 'two inventions' which, as Churchill explains, 'seemed a good idea at the time but were inadvertently poisonous' (*LGP* x). Midgley was played by the one performer who crossed disciplines by singing and speaking which, although a practical casting decision (*LGP* viii), underlined his ability to translocate.

Like *Traps*, *Poisoners* creates a 'reality' which can only exist on stage. While McDonald's design needed to set the worlds of Edwardian England, Ancient Greece and seventeenth-century France, it also indexed a trans-historical, trans-mythological world 'outside' of these (*LGP* xvii). As an abstract, three-walled design, it encoded a collapsing of boundaries – spaces which might be closed and open, private and public. As McDonald explains:

> We created interiors and exteriors, both open and private. Performers could appear above the walls or around them and in the gaps or corridors between walls They could be isolated in their own separate worlds and at the same time be overlooked by other performers. (*LGP* xvii–xviii)

In order to link rather than separate the three narratives, McDonald's design exploited the transformability of the theatrical sign. Not only did spaces transform into other spaces, but simple props were used as sign-vehicles to denote a number of different objects: a metal container, introduced in the Crippen sequence, was used first as his wife's jewel box and subsequently became the hat box containing her head. The same container was used again in the other two sections: 'as the vessel that held the poisoned wedding dress given to Creusa and then the casket of letters that contained the evidence that condemned Mme de Brinvilliers' (*LGP* xviii). The costuming of the performers also underlined continuity rather than difference. As McDonald explains, like the set, costumes were not period specific, but were designed 'to create a world of their own', and could be removed through 'the different sections of the story' (*LGP* xviii).

Transformability was also a feature of the distribution of roles. Performers did not so much triple-role-play through each of the three narratives, as transmute between different characters. For example, the female singer who played Crippen's wife Cora appears transformed at the end of the first sequence as Medea, and at the end of the second Medea sequence as Mme Brinvilliers. This initiates complex shifts in agency: the woman who is the poisoned victim (Cora) takes her revenge (Medea) and poisons, and is punished for poisoning (Brinvilliers). Similarly, the actor who played Crippen the poisoner, becomes Jason, victim of Medea's revenge, and in Section Three is Sainte-Croix, Brinvillier's lover. Shifts in agency are underpinned by the dangerous love-triangles which structure each section and initiate violent passions and violent deaths: Crippin poisons Cora because he desires Ethel; Medea poisons Creusa because of her passion for Jason, and Mme Brinvilliers poisons her husband in an attempt to secure her lover, Sainte-Croix (who complicates the third narrative by administering an antidote to Brinvilliers, refusing Mme Brinvilliers, and inadvertently poisoning himself through his own experiments). The triangular shaping of narrative action is echoed in McDonald's three-walled design, the use of three registers (dance, music, acting), and the three lives, three-sectioned structure of *Poisoners*.

That characters were not separate between 'worlds' but encoded traces of their former 'selves' was signed on and through the body in a variety of different ways. For instance, in the second narrative sequence Medea appears to lament over the 'rage' which consumes her: 'I'm the same Medea who cures the sick and brings the dead to life' (*LGP* 34). This was the Medea who was shown in the prologue giving 'life' to Aeson. Later we see Medea transformed into Brinvilliers, administering 'medicine' to the sick which poisons and kills them. The sung lines from the prologue are repeated but inverted: the power to 'heal' through 'hurting' (*LGP* 5) is transformed into the power to 'hurt' through 'healing' (*LGP* 41). It is the 'same' performer who embodies the antithesis to hurt and to heal. It is also the 'same' performer whose head is cut off by her husband in Section One (Cora), and is decapitated on a chopping block (the metal container from Section One) in Section Three (Brinvilliers).

Similarly, vocal and gestural registers are constantly traced across the different sections through the singers and dancers. The gestural imaging of Brinvillier's water torture in Section Three is described as *'reminiscent of Medea pouring potion into Aeson's throat'* (*LGP* 63), and the dancers playing the hospital patients poisoned by Brinvilliers die *'using movements reminiscent of the music hall characters'* (*LGP* 41) which they danced in the Crippen narrative. Cora's music hall song in Section One sings of the Brinvilliers story; the chorus lament for Creusa (*LGP* 37) is echoed in Mme de Sevigne's lyrics on the death of Brinvilliers (*LGP* 65). A game of whist in Crippen's story is used to play out sexual tensions between characters, and in Section Three, in a style reminiscent of Laclos's *Les liaisons dangereuses*, characters play the *'sexy, bitchy and increasingly savage'* game of Hoca (*LGP* 46), and so on. One dominant, repeated motif is the poisoning. The poisonings are not enacted through mimetic representation, but victims are sung and danced to death by a chorus of poisoners. This exemplifies the physicality of the stage language in *Poisoners* – a physicality not reserved just for the dancers, but for the overall concept, design and performance register of the piece.

One might be tempted to argue that the experimental form of *Poisoners* is in itself a sufficient 'purpose' for the piece (although some reviewers argued that this simply did not work),[32] but there are also significant, ideological concerns which unfold in the playing. The 'art' of poisoning is constantly referenced as an 'indetectable' means of administering harm. Like *A Mouthful of Birds, Poisoners* makes an 'unseen' or repressed 'truth' visible, demonstrating the dangerous reality of that which we cannot 'see'. *Poisoners* critiques our complicity in the often 'indetectable' ways in which we poison ourselves and our environment, and, importantly, the political fictions which are created to prevent us from seeing the harm we do to ourselves or is done to us.

This is powerfully encoded in Section Three when, in their laboratory, Sainte-Croix, Exili and La Chausee experiment with dangerous poisons in the interests of financial gain – to 'corner the market' (*LGP* 42). A fascinated Midgely watches and speaks of his own discovery of CFCs which he ironically proclaims to be 'non-toxic' (*LGP* 44). As the poisoners continue their experiments, the real danger of their work is exposed in a complex imaging in which M. Brinvilliers is being poisoned by his wife, and Mme Dufay is seen *'powdering herself and clouds of powder rise into the air'* (*LGP* 44). The 'clouds of powder' suggest the mushroom clouds of nuclear poisoning, linking the dangerous experiments to global disaster which affects us all. As Midgley comments, 'something strange is going on here. There's something in the air' (*LGP* 46). The scene continues with a self-poisoning motif as Mme de Sevigne sings of the 'rubbish . . . we rub on our faces', and Dufay and Sainte-Croix go *'into a face massage dance'* (*LGP* 46). This further links to the self-poisoning signed on the body through the costuming. McDonald explains, for example, how the cast used corsets 'on top of and underneath other garments' to create a 'visual symbol of how we poison ourselves for personal vanity' (*LGP* xviii).

After the death of Mme de Brinvilliers, Sainte-Croix serves coffee and amaretti to the assembled company. When the amaretti are unwrapped, the papers are rolled up, and Sainte-

Croix '*sets fire to them so that the burning paper floats up into the air and the ash floats down*' (*LGP* 65). Like the clouds of dusting powder, this is a powerful (nuclear) image of poisoning the world's atmosphere, underscored by Mme de Sevigne's lyrics which sing of Brinvilliers's poisoned body polluting the air for them all to breathe in. However, the lyrics also reference the body scattered in the air as a form of contagion; poisoning as a disease, a 'mania', which we all breathe in and are infected by.

This links to the political implications of poison as a harmful way of life. The third section uses the seventeenth-century world of immorality, greed and corruption as a means of historicizing the decadence of our own twentieth-century society. In a key speech by Sainte-Croix he states that the harm, the poison, is not just a matter of scandalous love affairs (although in 1990s Britain Tory ministers have given us enough of these), but that 'the whole political life of the country depends on poison' (*LGP* 58). It is a society in which as long as you have 'connections' you do not get punished for poisoning, for harmful acts, and in which everyone in 'public life' simply drinks a daily 'antidote' (*LGP* 58). The political lies go undetected.

In 1990s Britain, we are, perhaps, just beginning to see the unmasking of some of the political fictions which, for example, have denied that drugs issued to soldiers in the Falklands War may have 'poisoned' their bodies and those of their unborn children; that living under overhead power-lines may cause cancer, or, most recently, that BSE can 'poison' humans as well as cattle. As *Poisoners* demonstrates, left undetected, poisonous lies create dangerous, fatal realities.

'A MOUTHFUL OF WORDS': *THE SKRIKER*

Working collaboratively across disciplines tends to confound not only the critics but also the funding bodies, as evidenced during the tour of *Poisoners* when Second Stride found its Arts Council funding cut. As composer Judith Weir, who had previously worked with the company explained, 'Second Stride is a bureaucrat's nightmare no more; the inconvenient mix of dance, theatre, opera and mime, has lost its Arts Council grant'.[33] Not until 1994, therefore, did Churchill have the opportunity to collaborate again with Second Stride when, finally, they were able to work together on *The Skriker* which opened at the Cottesloe, Royal National Theatre, London (January 1994).

In an interview broadcast on the eve of the opening night, Churchill explained how, for the first time, she had sat down to write a play by herself and had ended up writing dance into it in the form of stage directions for dancers.[34] This was, therefore, a different way of working from other collaborative ventures, such as the Joint Stock productions which had had periods of workshopping and research. Churchill further clarified how, during the writing, she had made a decision to pare the central action of the play down to the three main figures – the Skriker and the two young girls, Josie and Lily – and to have the numerous stories and creatures which she had originally thought of weaving into plots and events, enacted in a different way: through dance and music.[35]

The central figure in Churchill's play is the Skriker, described as *'a shapeshifter and death portent, ancient and damaged'* (*TS* 1). As an 'ancient and damaged' figure of a mythological, folkloric, underworld, the Skriker haunts two young girls in the modern world. At the start of the play one girl, Josie, is in a mental institution for having apparently killed her baby daughter; the other, Lily, is pregnant and running away from home. As the Skriker attaches herself to the two girls, shapeshifting through a number of disguises, she tries to lure them both into the underworld of spirits. Josie is transported to the underworld and, after what seems like years there, is brought back to the modern world apparently seconds later. Lily, at the close of the play, leaves her baby in the modern world, believing that, like Josie, she too can be magicked away and back in seconds; but, instead, to her horror, she finds herself trapped in the future, ghastly 'real world' of her granddaughter and great-great-granddaughter.

Both worlds in *The Skriker*, the ancient and the modern, are represented as damaged. Damaged is, arguably, the dominant thematic, linguistic and stylistic register in the play. The underworld of the Skriker is figured as the damaged (Kristevan) semiotic: a marginal word inhabited by mis-

shapen, grotesque, spirit bodies whose 'monumental' config-
uration of time, space, reality, constantly border, press on the
'real'.[36] In performance, this is visually represented by Spink's
silent choreographing of the spirit world among the speaking
characters in the modern world, and further imaged in
sequences in which business men meet, unaware that they
have 'thrumpins' on their shoulders (*TS* 36), and a family picnic
takes place on a beach covered in 'blue men' (*TS* 48).[37]

The 'real', modern world which the Skriker and the spirits
haunt and punctuate is also damaged. Josie and Lily, as the two
main characters of the modern world are representative of a
non-represented, disempowered class. As young, working-class
women their 'future' is as oppressed and 'frightening' as
Angie's in *Top Girls,* or that of the teenage girls in *Fen.* Moreover,
their world is one which echoes the violent landscapes of
Icecream or the ecological disasters indexed in *Poisoners.* It is a
world which, as the Skriker describes, is damaged and poisoned
by war, drought, Aids, toxic waste (*TS* 31); in which 'nature'
which has always 'been a comfort to people as long as they've
existed', is 'not available any more' (*TS* 43).

If 'mother earth' is no longer life-sustaining, then neither are
the mother figures. Josie as a mother, a life-giver, has already
become a life-taker before the action begins. Lily, blasted away
from her 'rockabye baby gone the treetop' (*TS* 51) in the closing
apocalyptic vision, is left with the howling rage of her
daughter's progeny. If the play is 'read', as reviewers variously
claimed, as Churchill's way of exploring 'the anxious mood of
the nineties'; as 'a chilling look at life at the end of the
millennium',[38] then the theme of damaged motherhood may be
seen in this context as a specific anxiety of the 1990s; a decade in
which the right-wing, reactionary crusade against young, single
mothers, like Josie and Lily, remains unabated.[39]

Damaged motherhood and risk to the child (the future) is
further represented in *The Skriker* in a number of different ways.
It figures in the fragmented, corrupted lines from nursery
rhymes in the Skriker's speech. It is suggested in the narrative
fairytale encoding which plays against the traditional, structural
motif of the domestic world touched by good magic to bring
about a happy-ever-after ending, to show, instead, the mother
damaged, not rescued, hurtling towards destructive chaos.

Several of the spirits who haunt the playing space are those who are traditionally thought to prey on young children: Rawhea-dandBloodyBones, 'a nursery goblin who drags children down into marlpits or lurks in dark cupboards'; Jennie Greenteeth, 'a water fairy who drowns children'; Nellie Longarms 'a water spirit who drags children into ponds', and Black Annis who 'devours lambs and young children'.[40] The figure of a dead child sings of the mother who killed her and baked her in a pie to be eaten by her family (*TS* 19), and the Skriker is particularly concerned to get hold of Lily's baby.

The Skriker's obsession with Lily's baby is an expression of her need. As a figure, the Skriker constitutes a complex, contradictory meshing of transformative powers and a need of others. As Spink explained, 'the Skriker on the one hand seems to have endless powers to transform and to manipulate and to control things, yet at the same time has this desperate need to feed off people', adding that he thought this 'the most interesting character that she [Churchill] has ever written'.[41] To be needed, to be wanted, means that the Skriker must be recognized, be visible, be seen by others, whereas her shapeshifting power resides in invisibility. This duality is imaged in some of the Skriker's shapeshifting which takes the form of very needy figures – an old woman begging for money and affection, a young child needing to be mothered – and her invisible 'appearances'. For example, she becomes part of the sofa which seats Lily and Josie, from where she watches the girls unseen (*TS* 20), later making herself visible, 'leap[ing]' out of the sofa in the guise of a gaudy, Christmas fairy (*TS* 22). Her ability to appear and to disappear, her 'active vanishing',[42] gives her power over others; her need to be recognized authorizes power in others. In the 'invisible' spirit world, this is echoed in the silent imaging of the figure of a young girl with a telescope, who gazes on a Green Lady dancing with a Bogle and becomes sad when she can no longer 'see' them. As an unobserved observer of others, of whom she loses sight, the young girl's neediness is physically marked towards the close of the play when she enters with *'bandaged wrists'* (*TS* 49).

The constant play between visibility and invisibility links to the staging of the modern as visible and the mythological as invisible, not as discrete parallels but as interconnecting worlds.

The Skriker, who has known ancient, better times, when people were kinder to spirits and 'used to leave cream in a sorcerer's apprentice', is now damaged, 'poison[ed]' by a hateful and hurtful world (*TS* 4). Similarly, the maternal body is no longer nurtured, protected and cared for in the modern world. As young, single mothers, Josie and Lily are alone in the world. Josie's 'murder' of her young baby is, therefore, an example of how the 'damaged' maternal, in turn harms the child. Connections are further signed through the liminality of the Skriker's body which subverts the binarism of visibility and invisibility, and Lily's pregnant body: the visible, maternal body which carries the invisible child. Lily's experience of pregnancy is mirrored in Josie's experience of the monumental in the underworld, an event, which, as Josie explains to Lily was 'as big as that [pregnancy] is to you' (*TS* 37); and connecting worlds are imaged as Lily's shoe, which she kicks off by the sofa, is reproduced, larger than life, by the spirit world who dance around it (*TS* 41).

Moreover, time, space and reality are uncertain in both worlds. Lured to the underworld, Josie is tempted by the banquet of the spirits, which appears wonderful, but on closer inspection is shown to be '*not working – some of the food is twigs, leaves, beetles, some of the clothes are rags, some of the beautiful people have a claw hand or hideous face*' and the hostess, the Skriker, '*is a fairy queen, dressed grandiosely with lapses*' (*TS* 29). The fantastic feast turns to nightmare as Josie is trapped in the underworld and lives through a lifetime of misery in seconds. Similarly, Lily, in the modern world, is uncertain of what is real, what happens, what is a dream, a nightmare, a state of waking or a state of sleeping (*TS* 22). As in *Icecream*, there is a suggestion that the modern world is constituted by a series of projected images through which we lose touch with the 'real'. Lily, for example, called upon by the Skriker, disguised as an American woman, to explain the workings of television in a hotel bar, delivers a halting narrative of satellites beaming pictures around the world; the television image, a picture, is 'not a solid thing, it's all dots' (*TS* 14).

Lily's halting, broken narrative suggests a further linking of worlds, as her inexpressivity echoes the Skriker's damaged language. After the birth of her baby, for example, traces of the

Skriker's corrupted welcoming-the-baby clichés – 'happy birth to a baby a booby a babbly byebye booboo boohoo hoooooo. What a blossom bless'em' (*TS* 36) – are echoed in her speech:

> Everyone says you'll be tired or they...bunnies or fluffy...everything too sweet and you think that's really boring, makes you want to dress her in black but she's not sweet like pink and blue. Or you get them moaning about never get enough sleep or oh my stitches or like that, no one lets on. (*TS* 36)

The play's most striking example of linguistic deformation occurs in the Skriker's long, opening monologue, or as one reviewer described it 'a massive mouthful of words'.[43] For some critics it was Churchill's linguistic play which caught 'the memory', rather than the visual language of performance.[44] While reviewers invariably characterized the Skriker's fragmented, associative speech patterns as 'Joycean', Churchill herself likened the spirit's damaged language to the schizophrenic breakdown of language; language which the Striker is not entirely in control of.[45] Visually, the deformation was also encoded in the Skriker's distorted opening appearance: a 'spidery tangle of arms legs and black wings'.[46] Kathryn Hunter's physical gesturing as the Skriker was as deformed as her language. Her body, limbs, hands, feet, twisted into different spider-like shapes, underscored by the costuming: tufts of greying hair surrounding a face of deathly pallor, limbs banded in black and grey, and a shredded black bodice framed by moth-like wings. At the close of the opening monologue her spirit body, poised with open wings, twisted and turned on the threshold of flight, in conjunction with her linguistic outpouring:

> An open grave must be fed up you go like dust in the sunlight of heart. Gobble gobble says the turkey turnkey key to my heart, gobbledegook de gook is after you. Ready or not here we come quick or dead of night night sleep tightarse. (*TS* 581)

But, like Doreen in *A Mouthful of Birds* whose 'head is filled with horrible images' and whose mouth is choking with the 'feathers...blood...and broken bones' of birds (*MB* 71), the Skriker's body carries the memory of flight in a damaged form. In this respect it is significant that this spirit – 'not a major spirit but a spirit' – (*TS* 16) has a female body: a repressed body, damaged by an ancient past, birthing a catastrophic future.

Although the plays examined in this chapter show Churchill moving away from words into a language of performance, she also stressed at the time of *The Skriker* that she did not see herself 'abandon[ing] words entirely', that she would 'be just as likely to suddenly do a play with a lot of quite complicated text and no dance'.[47] A few months later she demonstrated her dramatic flexibility and on-going commitment to 'words' in her translation of Seneca's tragedy, *Thyestes,* which played at the Royal Court Theatre Upstairs. Her translation of the Roman revenge play resonates with contemporary concerns – as Churchill herself commented, 'the news seems full of revenge stories'.[48] Again, imaged in *Thyestes* is a world being poisoned, where 'river beds are empty' and natural resources are running out, and there is, Churchill explained, no optimistic, 'uplifting' chorus, Greek style. Instead 'the play ends bleakly except for our memory of a chorus who'd hoped for something better'.[49] As in *The Skriker,* the spectator is projected into a world – past, present and future – of global chaos.

The ability to move from the performance-based register of *The Skriker* to the emphasis on the linguistic in *Thyestes* is testimony to Churchill's versatility as a dramatist. Formally, Churchill has demonstrated a remarkable agility, working in a number of different styles, registers and disciplines, just as ideologically and politically she has not become locked into particular 'isms'. 'Her plays', as Judith Mackrell noted during rehearsals for *The Skriker,* 'differ so radically from each other' that 'you can't deduce from them a specific Churchill territory, a specific Churchill stance'.[50] If there is an underlying 'shape' to her theatre and an overall 'message', then perhaps these lie in Churchill's shapeshifting skills and interests; her ability to make visible to the spectator actual and potential dangers of an unequal, *man*made, damaged world, in which women are frequently figured as the most vulnerable and the most at risk.

Postscript – Fragments From a Diary: Two Revivals and *Hotel*

November 1996   The Royal National Theatre mount a mobile, touring production of *Light Shining in Buckinghamshire*, which plays the Cottesloe early in 1997. Directed by Mark Wing-Davey, whose work with Churchill most notably includes *Mad Forest* (see chapter 4), the revival of *Light Shining* is a critically acclaimed,[1] chilling and timely reminder of missed opportunities; failed revolutionary moments.

Saturday, 1 March 1997   To the Royal National Theatre to see *Light Shining*. On the concrete walkways and underpasses, the homeless and dispossessed beg from those of us in more fortunate and more comfortable circumstances; those of us who can afford to go to the theatre.

Outside the theatre the publicity poster for the production depicts two seventeenth-century costumed figures, one armed with a hand-held shovel, struggling uphill against modern, earth-excavating machinery, towering menacingly above them.

Inside the theatre, the set, austere and practical in design, suggests enclosure (metal railings), surveillance (a CCTV camera relays fragmented images of the performers on to a backcloth) and deprivation (the multi-location, multi-role-playing devices leave no one permanently 'owning' their own space; properties are sparse, minimal and functional). The programme notes include a specially commissioned piece by George Monbiot, founder of The Land Is Ours campaign,[2] and our attention is drawn to the parallels between the seventeenth-century Diggers who tried to claim land for ordinary people, and modern-day, twentieth-century protesters, fighting against homelessness and capitalist developers who put business before the environment.

Mid-March 1997 The images which remain after the production is gone are those which foreground the (currently ever widening) gap between the 'haves' and the 'have nots': the image of a golfer juxtaposed with the narration of ordinary people laying claim to land at St George's Hill in Surrey (now a golf course); the new landlord, Star, talking down to the Vicar from the height of his 'horse', and the woman who leaves her baby because she is too poor to feed it, her body too undernourished to provide milk. This last image is particularly vivid. The mother hesitates in front of a stand of lighted candles – the kind you can buy in a church to 'pay' for a prayer. Only she has no money for prayer; no food for her child.

Late March Headlining the news is the prospect of a general election. I reflect: *Light Shining* speaks 'frightening' truths about a government which has neither listened to, nor spiritually, culturally and materially cared for its 'children'.

Other, more delightful, news arrives of a new Churchill piece: *Hotel*. The Publisher obtains proofs from Nick Hern and calls a halt in the production process of this volume so that we can include a postscript on the new work. The programme notes arrive from Guy Chapman Associates. Music, singers, dancers – I realize it is a piece that has to be seen.

Nick Hern sends his 1997 theatre catalogue, announcing a new edition of *Light Shining* to coincide with the revival, and the promise of a third collection of plays for summer 1997, at the same time as a second new Churchill production, *Blue Heart*, is due to take place. This will bring Churchill back together with Max Stafford-Clark, now with the Out of Joint company.

Meanwhile, *Light Shining* completes its tour and the Peter Hall Company at the Old Vic, London, revive *Cloud Nine* as part of its seven-days-a-week repertory season of new and classic plays.

Sunday, 6 April 1997 I go to see the *Cloud Nine* revival. I think this must be my first experience of a Sunday matinée at a professional theatre.

If the concrete jungle of the National Theatre as a 'home' for the homeless was encoded in the production of *Light Shining in Buckinghamshire*, then the nineteenth-century architecture of the Old Vic brings a feel of the empire to Churchill's colonial critique in Act One of *Cloud Nine*. Watching from the (giddy) heights of the Baylis circle, and negotiating a view of the stage through the theatre's huge crystal chandelier, I feel as trapped as the family below me on their nineteenth-century colonial veranda (complete with stuffed leopard and huge elephant tusks).

Tracks of 1970s popular music (as diverse as Abba and the Sex Pistols) intersperse the playing of Act Two, and remind us of a past decade which also failed in its revolutionary promise (started in the 1960s) of sexual freedom. The park orgy scene in Act Two seems as remote to us now as the Ranters at the close of *Light Shining*, clinging to their belief in free love. That attitudes towards sexual politics have regressed rather than progressed since the writing of *Cloud Nine*, is heightened through the figure of Gerry, whose spectre-like haunting of the stage makes visible the (more recent) threat of Aids. The performer in this role works mostly apart from the group and in a different rhythm to the others: a slower, ghost-like movement. Gerry's monologue about having casual sex on a train is moved to the start of Act Two so that Aids and promiscuity overshadow the opening with the children in the play-centre. The effect of this is to jolt the spectator into an awareness of the homophobic prejudice and panic about gays and Aids in recent years – the ways in which homosexuality has again been viewed, to use Clive's words, as a 'disease more dangerous than diphtheria'.

A central failing of the Old Vic revival, however, is the inability of the company to develop and to sustain an ensemble style – a failing which serves to highlight the centrality of the collaborative and collective ethos to Churchill's theatre.

Tuesday, 22 April 1997 I am again reminded of the collaborative impulse of Churchill's theatre-making as *Hotel*, the first new piece since *The Skriker* and *Thyestes* in 1994, opens in London. As in the revival of *Light Shining in Buckinghamshire*, the ensemble playing in *Hotel* is quite brilliant.

Premièred at the Schauspielhaus in Hanover on 15 April 1997,

Hotel transfers to The Place Theatre London as part of the *Spring Loaded* dance festival. The piece renews Churchill's collaboration with Ian Spink, Orlando Gough and Second Stride. Directed and choreographed by Spink, Churchill's words for *Hotel* are set to Gough's music, and the piece, presented in two parts, is performed by thirteen singers, two dancers and three musicians.

The first part entitled 'Eight Rooms', portrays several different characters spending one night in a hotel. While there are six couples, and two single guests (a business man and a birdbook woman) staying at the hotel, the notional 'eight rooms' required to accommodate all of these characters, are played as one space. The characters treat the hotel room – in which we see a couch, a closet, a sink (with bathroom 'off'), and two beds – as their own, but without interacting with the other couples, or single guests.

The piece is structured out of typical over-night hotel rituals, from the moment of arrival and the customary room inspections, through the personal routines of freshening up, changing clothes, getting ready for bed, sleeping badly, and so on, to the routine of getting up and choosing a continental or full English breakfast. Finally, there is an instantly recognizable ritual: the business man comes back to pinch the hotel soap.

The simultaneous playing out of these hotel routines among the various guests needs to be seen in order to grasp its effectiveness, and, in particular, to see the potential for comedy. For example, the two beds, key pieces of furniture in a hotel setting, have, at different moments, to accommodate all of the various guests. As Ian Spink states in the programme notes:

> Eight Rooms began as a challenge. How do you fit fourteen hotel guests into one room? What happens when they all eventually go to bed? The potential for enormous traffic jams in such an intimate space seemed huge and fascinating. In rehearsal we were to discover that the simplest of acts, the cleaning of teeth, the hanging up of a dress, the reading of a magazine, demanded a relaxed yet rigorous precision when taking into account the thirteen other occupants of the space. (notes to *H.* programme)

Guests take up different sleeping positions on the beds, in various, constantly changing configurations. For example, in the fourth section, entitled 'Sleep', the 'silent couple' were framed either side by the 'US couple ', who made it seem only 'natural' to be going to bed with two strangers wedged in between them.

In addition to the hotel guests, there is also the 'figure' of the television, and a ghost who makes a brief appearance. Both of these roles were played by the same performer. In contrast to the sleepless cacophony of sounds and words which has gone before, the ghost introduces a moment of stillness, quiet, and an emotional plea to come 'into your sleep'... can't you hear/ can't you see/ it's me (*H.* 17). The playing out of intermittent snatches of television programmes and the flicking through channels remind us of how we use the television as background noise to counter the silence of a hotel room, rather than giving it our undivided attention, as we might do under different viewing circumstances at home.

Churchill's text for *Hotel* represents a new departure in her experimental approach to writing for the stage. Where characters might sing or speak to each other in *Lives of the Great Poisoners*, in *Hotel* Churchill's words are entirely sung. The words come in fragments: incomplete sentences, phatic utterances, odd words and sounds. Churchill explains her interest in finding out 'how little... the characters' had to 'say to let us know enough about them', clarifying that she 'decided there would be no complete sentences, just little chunks of what was said or thought, that could be absorbed first time round or in a repeat or even never' (*H.* programme notes). In composing the music, 'a fragmentary libretto', Gough explains that he could 'make the text into music, rather than being dragged along by the words' (*H.* programme notes).

In the second part of *Hotel*, entitled 'Two Nights', the company of singers takes on the role of a chorus, singing fragments from a diary found in a hotel room – fragments concerned with bodies disappearing, disappearances and invisibility. The chorus appear and disappear within the set: still the hotel room, but with much of the furniture removed (to make a space for the dancers), and with cracks and apertures in the walls (a 'stripe' in the wallpaper comes out at an angle to create an opening, for instance), for unexplained entrances and exits. Two dancers, one male and one female, each have their own choreographed pieces which seem to connect with the theme of disappearance, but, like the diary fragments, remain unexplained and mysterious. The tone is altogether darker: the music has become oppressive and sinister, and the dancers encode narratives of isolation and desolation, in contrast to the collectively shared ritual of inconsequential hotel routines of the first part. The woman dancer, for example, variously appears in a blood-stained nurse's uniform, white underwear, a black plastic (prostitute's?) outfit, and a red evening dress. She handles a small pistol, and is handed (by the chorus) an even bigger gun. While the woman seems to want to lose herself in playing with sinister identities, trying them on and taking them off, the male dancer continues with some of the hotel rituals seen in the first part (an energetic dance routine centred on brushing the teeth, for example), but with hints of suicide narrative. As the piece ends, he is imaged alone, in a state of collapse, possibly dead, by the toilet at the back of the stage.

Thursday, 24 April 1997   Reviews of *Hotel* appear in the theatre columns in the national press (much preoccupied yesterday, the day after *Hotel*'s opening, with the revival of Brecht's *The Caucasian Chalk Circle* at the National). These are mostly favourable, with a preference for the first rather than the second part. Judith Mackrell contrasts 'the wonderful vigour of the first half ' to the second which 'ends not with mystery but with a feeling of arbitrariness'.[3] Paul Taylor feels 'you couldn't feel alienating pressure from the surrounding life of the hotel' in the second part,[4] although Benedict Nightingale, puzzling over the 'darker' second section, concludes, 'after a couple of days in some modern hotels, I can share graveyard feelings like those'.[5]

Thursday, 1 May 1997   The nation goes to the polls. *Hotel* opened within a week of the general election. Churchill's critique of the damage of a capitalist society, and the way its ideology creates the alienation we see in *Hotel*, goes far deeper and wider than criticism of a particular government. That is why her work will continue to be important.

Notes

CHAPTER 1. BEGINNINGS: RADIO, STAGE AND TELEVISION

1 Churchill, quoted in Judith Thurman, 'The Playwright Who Makes you Laugh about Orgasm, Racism, Class Struggle, Homophobia, Woman-Hating, the British Empire, and the Irrepressible Strangeness of the Human Heart', *Ms.*, May 1982, 51–7; 54.

2 Geraldine Cousin interview, *New Theatre Quarterly* Vol. IV, no. 13 (February 1988), 3–16; 3.

3 Ibid.

4 Ibid., 4.

5 Thurman, *Ms.*, May 1982, 51, 54.

6 Ibid., 51.

7 See chronology for details of early performed work. For details of early unperformed work, see Linda Fitzsimmons, *File on Churchill* (London: Methuen, 1989), 10–12.

8 Churchill, however, has stated that she was not aware of Freud's study at the time of writing. See Amelia Howe Kritzer, *The Plays of Caryl Churchill: Theatre of Empowerment* (Basingstoke: Macmillan, 1991), 202, n. 17.

9 Hélène Cixous, 'The Laugh of the Medusa', in Elaine Marks and Isabelle de Courtivron (eds), *New French Feminisms* (Brighton: Harvester, 1981), 245–64; 245.

10 Kritzer, 33. *The Female Malady* (London: Virago, 1987) is Elaine Showalter's study of women and madness.

11 Kritzer, 36.

12 Churchill cites chapter 5 of Fanon's *The Wretched of the Earth* (Harmondsworth: Penguin, 1967) as a reference point (S. 96).

13 *Black Skins, White Masks* is the title of a later study by Fanon, published in 1967. Churchill states that this 'was one of the things (along with Genet) that led to Joshua, the black servant, being played by a white in *Cloud Nine*' (S. Intro).

14 R. D. Laing, *The Divided Self* (1960; Harmondsworth: Penguin/ Pelican, 1965), 181.

15 On the rhetoric of the starving body as guilt, imperialism and war, see Maud Ellman on Jane Fonda's Keep Fit programme and diet as response to the Vietnam War in *The Hunger Artists* (London: Virago, 1993), 9–11.

16 In *Top Girls* Angie puts on a dress which is now too small for her, but which is significant because it was given to her by her real mother, Marlene, in order, she states, 'to kill my mother' (*P2* 98).

17 Quoted in Fitzsimmons, 18.

18 Jackie Kay interview, *New Statesman and Society*, 21 April 1989, 41–2; 42.

19 See my *An introduction to Feminism and Theatre* (London: Routledge, 1995), 143.

CHAPTER 2. THE 'WOMAN WRITER'

1 Ann McFerran 'The Theatre's (Somewhat) Angry Young Women', *Time Out*, 28 October–3 November 1977, 13–15.

2 Gillian Hanna, introduction to *Monstrous Regiment: A Collective Celebration* (London: Nick Hern, 1991), xxvii–xxix.

3 McFerran, 13.

4 Ibid.

5 Ibid., 15.

6 Churchill in 'Caryl Churchill', in Kathleen Betsko and Rachel Koenig (eds), *Interviews with Contemporary Women Playwrights*, (New York: Beech Tree Books, 1987), 75–84; 76.

7 For plot descriptions of these two unpublished plays, see Geraldine Cousin, *Churchill the Playwright*, (London: Methuen, 1989), 107–9.

8 See Sue-Ellen Case, *Feminism and Theatre* (Basingstoke: Macmillan, 1988), chapter 7, 'Towards a New Poetics', for an overview of developments in feminist theory, film and performance.

9 Churchill in 'Caryl Churchill, author of this month's playtext, talks to p & p', *Plays and Players*, January 1973, 40 and p. 1 of special inset publishing script of *Owners*; 40.

10 Ibid.

11 *Plays and Players*, February 1973, 41–2; 42.

12 Ibid.

13 *Plays and Players*, January 1973, inset p. 1.

14 Hélène Cixous and Catherine Clément. *The Newly Born Woman* (Manchester: Manchester University Press, 1987), 78.

15 Ibid. 80. On the mastery of women by men see also Eva Figes, *Patriarchal Attitudes* (1970; London: Faber and Faber, 1978), which Churchill states she had read not long before the writing of *Owners* and 'which may have affected the character of Clegg' (*P1* 4).

16 Phyllis Chesler, *Sacred Bond: Motherhood Under Siege* (London: Virago, 1990), 122.

17 The Baby M case took place in the mid-1980s when Mary Beth Whitehead agreed to be paid to give birth to a baby for William and Elizabeth Stern. She changed her mind after the birth, which gave rise to a highly publicized court battle in which she, as the birth mother, lost her rights to the child.

18 For further discussion of this point, see Peggy Phelan on 'White men and pregnancy: discovering the body to be rescued', in *Unmarked* (London: Routledge, 1993), 130–45.

19 See, for example, Adrienne Rich, *of Woman Born* (London: Virago, 1977).

20 The Channel 4 documentary *The Dying Rooms*, broadcast in 1995, revealed the appalling conditions of orphanages which house the abandoned girl children of China.

21 The natural resources issue was pressing in the early 1970s, culminating in the oil crisis in 1973, but, arguably, matters of ecology have become even more pressing in recent years with the concern for global warming, the destruction of the rain forests, the continued abuse of other natural resources, and so on. It remains an urgent issue in Churchill's theatre; see, for example discussion of plays in Chapter 5.

22 *New Statesmen and Society*, 21 April 1989, 41.

23 Churchill, quoted in Catherine Itzin, *Stages in the Revolution* (London: Methuen, 1980), 282.

24 Churchill in McFerran's interview, 13.

25 Quoted in Elaine Aston (ed.), *Feminist Theatre Voices: A Collective Oral History* (Loughborough: Loughborough Theatre Texts, 1997), 70.

26 Churchill interview in Betsko and Koenig (eds), 77.

27 David Zane Mairowitz, 'God and the Devil', *Plays and Players*, February 1977, 24–5; 25.

28 Ibid.

29 *Spare Rib*, December 1976, 38.

30 *The Times*, 8 December 1976, 11.

31 Gillian Hanna, *Feminism and Theatre*, Theatre Papers, 2nd series, no. 8 (Dartington, Devon: Dartington College, 1978), 9.

32 Wandor, *Spare Rib*, 1976, 38.

33 Clément, in Cixous and Clément, 8.

34 Ibid., 7.

35 For an overview of Irigaray's speculum, see Toril Moi, *Sexual/Textual Politics: Feminist Literary Theory* (London: Routledge, 1985), 127–31.

36 Hanna, 1978, 9–10.

37 Reported in the *Guardian*, 'Home News' section, 12 October 1993, 2.

38 Michèle Roberts, review of *Floorshow, Spare Rib*, January 1978, 38.

39 Churchill, *Omnibus*, BBC1, November 1988.

40 Sue-Ellen Case and Jeanie K. Forte, 'From Formalism to Feminism', *Theater* 16 (1985), 62–5; 65.

41 Elizabeth Grosz, *Volatile Bodies: Toward a Corporeal Feminism* (Bloomington and Indianapolis: Indiana University Press, 1994), 199.

42 Susan Carlson, 'Comic Collisions: Convention, Rage, and Order', *New Theatre Quarterly*, 12 (November 1987), 303–16; 313.

43 Antony Sher in Rob Ritchie, (ed.), *The Joint Stock Book* (London: Methuen, 1987), 139–40. For further details of the workshopping and rehearsal processes see Michelene Wandor, 'Free Collective Bargaining', in *Time Out*, 30 March–5 April 1979, 14-16.

44 Lynne Truss interview, *Plays and Players*, January 1984, 8–10; 10.

45 John Simon interview, *Vogue*, August 1983, 126 and 130; 126.

46 *Plays and Players*, May 1979, 23.

47 Quoted in Thurman, *Ms.*, May 1982, 54,

48 Lynne Truss interview, *Plays and Players*, January 1984, 8.

49 Ibid.

50 Written in 1979, performed in 1980 at the Soho Poly, and published in *Churchill: Shorts*, 245–73.

51 Elin Diamond, '(In)Visible Bodies in Churchill's Theater', in Lynda Hart (ed.), *Making a Spectacle* (Ann Arbor: University of Michigan Press, 1989), 259–81; 266.

52 *Plays and Players*, November 1982, 22–3; 23.

53 Sue-Ellen Case, *Feminism and Theatre*, 87.

54 Pat Barr's study of Isabella Bird, *A Curious Life for a Lady* (London: Secker & Warburg, 1970), which Churchill used as background research for *Top Girls*, also notes that Hennie (like Joyce), in contrast to Isabella (like Marlene), satisfied a maternal need by looking after and educating a young girl from their village.

55 Joseph Marohl, 'De-realised Women: Performance and Identity in *Top Girls*', *Modern Drama*, vol. 30, no. 3 (September 1987), 376–88; 377.

56 *Plays and Players*, May 1991, 25.

57 See Susan Faludi's *Backlash* (London: Vintage, 1991 and 1992).

58 For details, see Fitzsimmons, *File on Churchill*, 8.

59 Quoted in *Feminist Theatre Voices*, 69.

60 Christopher Innes, *Modern British Drama 1890–1990* (Cambridge: Cambridge University Press, 1992), argues that Churchill and Pam Gems are 'the two major women writers whose work has become an important and influential part of the general repertoire' (p. 452). However, he claims that this was achieved by the women dramatists 'distanc[ing] themselves from the radical and more

subjective side of the feminist movement' (ibid.), whereas I would argue that, in Churchill's case, it is the radicalism of her writing, both formally and ideologically, which has exceptionally secured her a place in the modern dramatic canon.

CHAPTER 3. THE DRAMATIST AS SOCIALIST CRITIC

1 Churchill, *Omnibus*, BBC1, November 1988.
2 Quoted in Thurman, *Ms.*, May 1982, 51–7; 54.
3 Ibid.
4 Churchill, *The Ants*, in *New English Dramatists*, vol. 12 (Harmondsworth: Penguin, 1969), 89–103; 103.
5 Ibid.
6 *Moving Clocks Go Slow* remains unpublished, but for a description and analysis of the play, see Kritzer, 1991, 67–72.
7 *Sunday Times*, 5 January 1975, 30.
8 For production photographs of the set, see *Plays and Players*, March 1975, 24–5.
9 Ibid., 25.
10 Hannah Arendt, *On Violence* (London: Penguin, 1970), 67.
11 *The Times*, 3 January 1975, 7.
12 Ibid.
13 *Sunday Times*, 5 January 1975, 7.
14 *Plays and Players*, March 1975, 25.
15 Ronald Hayman interview with Caryl Churchill and Max Stafford-Clark, *Sunday Times Magazine*, 2 March 1980, 25–7; 27.
16 Ibid.
17 In Rob Ritchie, (ed.), *The Joint Stock Book*, 119.
18 *Sunday Times Magazine*, 2 March 1980, 27.
19 *The Times*, 28 September 1976, 20.
20 *Plays and Players*, February 1977, 24.
21 Elin Diamond, 'Brechtian Theory / Feminist Theory', *The Drama Review*, vol. 32, no. 1 (Spring 1988), 82–94; 87.
22 Ibid.
23 Ibid.
24 *The Times*, 28 September 1976, 20.
25 Eva Figes, *Patriarchal Attitudes* (London: Virago, 1970, revised 1978), 9.
26 *The After-Dinner Joke* is published in *Churchill: Shorts* 165–221, and is a further example of the renewed topicality of Churchill's early work: charity as big business in our era of Live Aid, Comic Relief, and so on.
27 For details see Catherine Itzin, *Stages in the Revolution*, 280–1.

28 Lynne Truss interview, *Plays and Players*, January 1984, 10.
29 *Times Literary Supplement*, 20 January 1984, 62.
30 *New Statesman*, 27 January 1984, 30–1.
31 *Guardian*, 11 January 1984, 9.
32 On the crowd as performer, and the unpredictibility of crowd response, see Michel Foucault, *Discipline and Punish*, translated by Alan Sheridan (Harmondsworth: Penguin, 1977) 57–69.
33 Churchill underlined this point in her introduction to the play in 1985, when she commented 'as this edition goes to press, the Government are attempting to depoliticise the miners and the rioters by emphasising a "criminal element"' (P2 3).
34 Giles Gordon, *Spectator*, 21 January, 27–8; 28.
35 Foucault, *Discipline and Punish*, 25.
36 Ibid.
37 *Times Literary Supplement*, 20 January 1984, 62. For a production photograph of this scene, see Ros Asquith's review in *City Limits*, 20–26 January 1984, 48.
38 Jane Thomas, 'The Plays of Caryl Churchill: Essays in Refusal', in Adrian Page, (ed.), *The Death of the Playwright?* (Basingstoke: Macmillan, 1992), 160–85; 169–70.
39 Janelle Reinelt, *After Brecht* (Ann Arbor: University of Michigan Press, 1994), 96.

CHAPTER 4. COMMUNITIES IN DRAMATIC DIALOGUE

1 See Select Bibliography, 'Source material for plays', for details of sources relating to certain of the plays studied in this volume.
2 Mary Chamberlain, *Fenwomen: A Portrait of Women in an English Village* (1975; London: Routledge & Kegan Paul, 1983).
3 See Chamberlain, 112–14.
4 Ibid., 3.
5 Ibid., 2–3.
6 *Omnibus*, BBC1, November 1988.
7 Explained by the director of *Fen*, Les Waters, ibid.
8 *Plays and Players*, October 1983, 39–40; 40.
9 Liz Bale, 'Everyday Life', *Spare Rib,* July 1984, 50–3; 52.
10 Chamberlain, 11–12.
11 Beverly Hayne, *Sunday Times Magazine*, 24 July 1983, 31.
12 *Omnibus*, BBC1, November 1988.
13 Peter Lewis, *The Times*, 30 June 1987, 9.
14 Explained in the programme notes for the West End, Wyndham's production.
15 *The Times*, 30 June 1987, 9.

16   John Peter, *Sunday Times*, 29 March 1987, 51.

17   Janelle Reinelt, *After Brecht*, 97.

18   Churchill, 'Driven by Greed and Fear', *New Statesman*, 17 July 1987, 10–11; 10.

19   Clare Colvin, *Plays and Players*, May 1987, 14.

20   *The Times*, 30 June 1987, 9.

21   *The Times*, 7 July 1987, 18.

22   *The Times*, 30 June 1987, 9.

23   Ruby Cohn, *Retreats from Realism in Recent English Drama* (Cambridge: Cambridge University Press, 1991), 91.

24   *Serious Money* made £14,000 a week for the Royal Court, which generated the funds for the West End transfer to Wyndham's. See *The Times*, 30 June 1987, 9. It is *Cloud Nine*, however, which is reported to be Churchill's 'biggest earner'. See Claire Armistead, 'Tale of the Unexpected', *Guardian*, Section 2, Arts, 12 January 1994, 4–5; 5.

25   Details explained by Reva Klein in *Times Education Supplement*, 29 June 1990, 35.

26   Jim Hiley interview, *The Times*, 10 October 1990, 25

27   *The Times*, 26 June 1990, 18.

28   Janelle Reinelt, *After Brecht*, 103.

29   Jeremy Kingston, *The Times*, 11 October 1990, 26.

30   Ibid.

31   *The Times*, 10 October 1990, 25.

CHAPTER 5. EXPLODING WORDS AND WORLDS

1   Churchill, 'Not Ordinary, Not Safe: A Direction for Drama?', *Twentieth Century*, November 1960, 443–51; 446.

2   Ibid.

3   W. Stephen Gilbert, *Plays and Players*, March 1977, 33.

4   *The Times*, 28 January 1977, 9.

5   *Spare Rib*, October 1986, 33.

6   For details, see Fitzsimmons, *File on Churchill*, 68–70.

7   See Geraldine Cousin interview, *New Theatre Quarterly*, February 1988, 6.

8   Churchill, 'Legend of a Woman Possessed', *Guardian*, 21 November 1986, 17.

9   *Spare Rib*, October 1986, 33.

10   For a development of this point, see Elin Diamond, '(In)visible Bodies in Churchill's Theatre', 277–8.

11   Churchill had earlier developed the motif of a woman with the power of flight, the power to move objects in the unperformed

stage play *Seagulls* (1978), published in *Churchill: Shorts*, 223–43. In *Seagulls* it is the loss of this power which is dramatized as the central issue, and, as Churchill explains in the introduction to *Churchill: Shorts*, this made the play feel like 'it was about not being able to write for me to want it done at the time'.

12 Michel Foucault, introduction to *Herculine Barbin,* translated by Richard McDougall (New York: Pantheon, 1980), vii.

13 Ibid.

14 Irving Wardle, *The Times,* 28 November 1986, 13.

15 Ann Fitzgerald, *Plays and Players*, November 1986, 33.

16 *Guardian*, 29 November 1986, 14.

17 Michael Coveney noted that 'the pattern of the piece [*Icecream*] reminds me of earlier plays like *Traps* and *Owners'* (*Financial Times*, 12 April 1989, 23).

18 See commentary by Kevin Jackson, in interview with Churchill, *Independent*, 12 April 1989, 15.

19 Michael Coveney noted that this actually happened to 'the American director Alan Schneider at Hampstead Theatre a few years back', *Financial Times*, 12 April 1989, 23.

20 *The Times*, 12 April 1989, 21.

21 Kevin Jackson interview, *Independent*, 12 April 1989, 15.

22 Ibid.

23 Janelle G. Reinelt and Joseph R. Roach, (eds), *Critical Theory and Performance* (Ann Arbor: University of Michigan Press, 1992), 1.

24 Ibid.

25 Suzanne Moore, 'New Meanings for New Markets', *Women's Review*, April 1987, 26–7; 26.

26 *Independent,* 12 April 1989, 15.

27 *Guardian*, 11 April 1989, 45.

28 Ibid.

29 Churchill, *Independent*, 12 April 1989, 15.

30 For a further example of Churchill using film as an escape from reality, see her short 1980 play *Three More Sleepless Nights*, (S 245–73). In this drama, Pete's monosyllabic girlfriend, Dawn, commits suicide in their shared bed, while he escapes from their inability to communicate by relating movie narratives – in particular, episodes from the science fiction film *Aliens*.

31 Churchill, interview, *New Statesman and Society*, 21 April 1989, 41–2; 42.

32 See, for example, John Percival's review in *The Times*, (14 March 1991, 22), where he argues that production did not 'make up its mind what it is doing', and that potential lines of development were, in his view, 'lost in a morass of silly ideas and fancy theatrical posturing in different modes'. Generally, more favourable review-

ing came from dance critics. See, for example, Judith Mackrell's review, *Independent*, 16 March 1991, 32.

33 *Guardian*, 15 March 1991, 37.

34 Interview, *Late Theatre*, BBC2, January 1994.

35 Ibid.

36 For an explanation of the Kristevan semiotic, marginal and monumental, see my, *An Introduction to Feminism and Theatre*, 51–6.

37 Programme notes for *The Skriker* give explanations for the various different kinds of spirits. A thrumpin is explained as 'a kind of attendant demon, believed to haunt every man with the power of taking his life'; blue men 'wreck ships unless the captain can outwit them at rhyming games'.

38 Gwyn Morgan, *Plays and Players*, February 1994, 5.

39 See page 30 of the present study for related discussion of this issue in section on *Vinegar Tom*.

40 Explanations are from the programme notes to *The Skriker*.

41 *Late Theatre*, BBC2, January 1994.

42 I take the phrasing from Peggy Phelan's *Unmarked* (p. 19).

43 Paul Taylor, *Independent*, 29 January 1994, 52.

44 See Malcolm Rutherford's review, *Weekend Financial Times*, January 29–30, 1994, xxii.

45 *Late Theatre*, BBC2, January 1994.

46 Benedict Nightingale, *The Times*, 29 January 1994, 16.

47 *Late Theatre*, BBC2, January 1994.

48 Churchill, *Thyestes* (London: Nick Hern, 1995), xiii. In particular, the news was dominated by the internecine fighting and revenge killings in Rwanda.

49 Ibid.

50 'Flights of Fancy', *Independent*, Arts Section, 20 January 1994, 25.

POSTSCRIPT – FRAGMENTS FROM A DIARY: TWO REVIVALS AND *HOTEL*

1 See Fiachra Gibbons, 'on the new relevance of Caryl Churchill's play *Light Shining in Buckinghamshire*', *Guardian*', 11 January 1997, 6.

2 For details of The Land Is Ours campaign, see 'Up in Smoke' by John Vidal and George Monbiot, *Guardian*, 16 October 1996, 1–3.

3 *Guardian*, 24 April 1997, 2.

4 *Independent*, 24 April 1997, 19.

5 *The Times*, 24 April 1997, 37.

Select Bibliography

PLAYS BY CHURCHILL

The Ants, in *New English Dramatists, vol. 12*, (Harmondsworth: Penguin, 1969), 89–103.

Churchill: Plays One – Owners, Traps, Vinegar Tom, Light Shining in Buckinghamshire, Cloud Nine (London: Methuen, 1985). Includes introduction and notes on individual plays by Churchill.

Objections to Sex and Violence, in *Plays by Women, vol. 4* (London: Methuen, 1985), 11–53. Includes Afterword by Churchill.

A Mouthful of Birds, with David Lan (London: Methuen, 1986). Includes Churchill's notes on the workshop and the play.

Icecream (London: Nick Hern, 1989).

Churchill: Plays Two – Softcops, Top Girls, Fen, Serious Money (London: Methuen, 1990). Includes introduction and notes on individual plays by Churchill.

Churchill: Shorts – Three More Sleepless Nights, Lovesick, The After-Dinner Joke, Abortive, Schreber's Nervous Illness, The Judge's Wife, The Hospital at the Time of the Revolution, Hot Fudge, Not Not Not Not Not Enough Oxygen, Seagulls (London: Nick Hern, 1990). Includes introduction and notes on individual plays by Churchill.

Mad Forest (London: Nick Hern, 1990; revised 1991).

Lives of the Great Poisoners (London: Methuen, 1993). Production dossier with introductions by Churchill and principal collaborators.

The Skriker (London: Nick Hern, 1994).

Thyestes, Seneca, translated by Churchill (London: Nick Hern, 1995). Includes introduction detailing Churchill's approach to translation.

Hotel, with Second Stride (London: Nick Hern, 1997).

SOURCE MATERIAL FOR PLAYS

Sources which Churchill identifies as influencing, or indeed directly

118

shaping her theatre, offer excellent ways into both academic study and practical exploration of her work. The following is a list of a number of the plays, together with some sources of background material.

Cloud Nine
Fanon, Frantz, *Black Skin, White Masks*, (New York: Grove Press, 1967). On colonialism.
Genet, Jean. His theatre, for colonialism and gender oppression.
Millett, Kate, *Sexual Politics* (1970; London: Virago, 1977).

Fen
Chamberlain, Mary, *Fenwomen: A Portrait of Women in an English Village* (1975; London: Routledge & Kegan Paul, 1983).

The Hospital at the Time of the Revolution
Fanon, Frantz, *The Wretched of the Earth,* translated by Constance Farrington (Harmondsworth: Penguin, 1967). On colonialism.
Laing, R. D., *The Divided Self* (1960; Harmondsworth: Penguin/Pelican, 1965). On schizophrenia.

Light Shining in Buckinghamshire
Churchill, Caryl, *Plays One*, p. 189, gives a list of documentary materials used in the play.

Lives of the Great Poisoners
Stokes, Hugh, *Mme de Brinvilliers and Her Times, 1630–1676* (London: John Lane, 1912), and see Churchill, *Lives of the Great Poisoners*, p. ix, for details of epistolary material consulted.

A Mouthful of Birds
Euripides, *The Bacchae* (Harmondsworth: Penguin, 1954).
McDougall, Richard, translator, *Herculine Barbin: Being the Recently Discovered Memoirs of a Nineteenth-Century French Hermaphrodite*, with introduction by Michel Foucault (New York: Pantheon Books, 1980).

Objections to Sex and Violence
Arendt, Hannah, *On Violence* (London: Penguin, 1970).

Owners
Figes, Eva, *Patriarchal Attitudes* (1970, London: Faber & Faber, 1978). On women's oppression.

Schreber's Nervous Illness
Schreber, Daniel Paul, *Memoirs of My Nervous Illness*, edited and translated by Ida Macalpine and Richard A. Hunter (London: William Dawson & Sons, 1955).

Serious Money
Shadwell, Thomas, *The Volunteers, or the Stock-Jobbers* (London, 1693).

The Skriker
Briggs, Mary Katharine, *The Fairies in Tradition and Literature* (London: Routledge & Kegan Paul, 1967). On folklore and folktales.

Softcops
Foucault, Michel, *Discipline and Punish*, translated by Alan Sheridan (Harmondsworth: Penguin, 1977).

Top Girls
Barr, Pat, *A Curious Life for a Lady* (London: Secker & Warburg, 1970). On Isabella Bird.

Brazell, Karen, translator, *The Confessions of Lady Nijo* (New York: Anchor Books, 1973). On Lady Nijo.

Vinegar Tom
Ehrenreich, Barbara, and Deidre English, *Witches, Midwives and Nurses* (New York: Feminist Press, 1973). On witchcraft and women as healers.

INTERVIEWS

Betsko, Kathleen and Rachel Koenig (eds), 'Caryl Churchill', *Interviews with Contemporary Women Playwrights* (New York: Beech Tree Books, 1987), 75–84. Has detail on *Top Girls*, *Fen*, *Cloud Nine* and working method with Joint Stock.

Cousin, Geraldine, 'The Common Imagination and the Individual Voice', *New Theatre Quarterly*, vol. IV, no. 13, February 1988, 3–16. Churchill talks about her career and plays. Discusses *A Mouthful of Birds* and *Serious Money* in detail.

Gooch, Steve, 'Caryl Churchill, author of this month's playtext, talks to p & p', *Plays and Players,* January 1973, 40, and p. 1 of script inset (the issue contains the complete script of *Owners*). Mainly about *Owners.*

Gussow, Mel, 'Caryl Churchill: A Genteel Playwright with an Angry Voice', *New York Times*, 22 November 1987, 1, 26. Interview during run of *Serious Money.*

Hayman, Ronald, 'Partners: Caryl Churchill and Max Stafford-Clark', *Sunday Times Magazine*, 2 March 1980, 25–7. On workshopping with Joint Stock.

Hiley, Jim, 'Revolution in Miniature', *The Times*, 10 October 1990, 25. Churchill talks about *Mad Forest.*

Jackson, Kevin, 'Incompatible Flavours', *Independent*, 12 April 1989, 15. On *Icecream.*

Kay, Jackie, 'Interview with Caryl Churchill', *New Statesman and Society*, 21 April 1989, 41–2. Churchill talks about her career in the theatre, audience reactions to *Serious Money*, and the production of *Icecream*.

Late Theatre, 'Interview with Churchill', BBC2, broadcast January 1994. Churchill talks about the production of *The Skriker*. Includes footage of *The Skriker* in rehearsal.

McFerran, Ann, 'The Theatre's (Somewhat) Angry Young Women', *Time Out*, 28 October–3 November 1977, 13–15. Discussion with contemporary women playwrights including Churchill.

Mackrell, Judith, 'Flights of Fancy', *Independent*, 20 January 1994, 25. Interview during rehearsal of *The Skriker*.

Omnibus on Caryl Churchill, BBC1, broadcast November 1988. Excellent documentary combining interview footage with performed extracts by Joint Stock/Royal Court players.

Simon, John, 'Sex, Politics, and Other Play Things', *Vogue,* August 1983, 126, 130. Includes discussion of *Top Girls*, *Fen* and workshopping of *Cloud Nine*.

Truss, Lynne, 'A Fair Cop', *Plays and Players*, January 1984, 8–10. Details *Softcops*.

STUDIES OF CHURCHILL'S WORK

Full-Length Studies

Cousin, Geraldine, *Churchill The Playwright* (London: Methuen, 1989). Very descriptive approach. Useful for plot summaries of early unpublished work.

Fitzsimmons, Linda (compiler), *File on Churchill* (London: Methuen, 1989). Contains synopses of plays and review material.

Kritzer, Amelia Howe, *The Plays of Caryl Churchill: Theatre of Empowerment* (Basingstoke: Macmillan, 1991). Detailed study which makes good use of critical theory and criticism to frame analysis.

Randall, Phyllis R. (ed.), *Caryl Churchill: A Casebook* (London and New York: Garland, 1988). Useful to dip in to. Bibliography offers explanatory framings for further reading suggestions.

Essays and Articles

Armitstead, Claire, 'Tale of the Unexpected', *Guardian*, Section 2, Arts, 12 January 1994, 4–5. Article written while *The Skriker* in rehearsal. Looks back over Churchill's career and profiles her current interest in dance-drama work. Some direct quotation of Churchill included.

Burk, Julie Thompson, 'Top Girls and the Politics of Representation', in Ellen Donkin and Susan Clement (eds), *Upstaging Big Daddy: Directing Theater as if Gender and Race Matter* (Ann Arbor: University of Michigan Press, 1993), 67–78. On directing a production of *Top Girls*.

Carlson, Susan, 'Comic Collisions: Convention, Rage, and Order', *New Theatre Quarterly*, vol. 3, no. 12, November 1987, 303–16. Has section on Churchill's play with comic conventions in *Cloud Nine*.

Chambers, Colin, and Mike Prior, 'Caryl Churchill: Women and the Jigsaw of Time', in *Playwrights' Progress: Patterns of Postwar British Drama* (Oxford: Amber Lane Press, 1987), 189–98. Surveys Churchill's career in context of male-dominated tradition of British drama.

Churchill, Caryl, 'Not Ordinary, Not Safe: A Direction for Drama?', *The Twentieth Century*, November 1960, 443–51.

———— 'Driven By Greed and Fear', *New Statesman*, 17 July 1987, 10–11. Churchill on the City and *Serious Money*.

———— on workshopping *Light Shining in Buckinghamshire* in, Ritchie, 118–21.

Cornish, Roger, and Violet Ketels (eds), 'Caryl Churchill' in *Landmarks of Modern British Drama: The Plays of the Seventies* (London: Methuen, 1986, 525–31). Survey and introduction to *Top Girls* (also published in the volume).

Diamond, Elin, '(In)Visible Bodies in Churchill's Theater', in Lynda Hart (ed.), *Making a Spectacle: Feminist Essays on Contemporary Women's Theatre* (Ann Arbor: University of Michigan Press, 1989), 259–81. Excellent theoretically informed essay which looks at the body and issues of representation, detailing *Fen* and *A Mouthful of Birds*.

———— 'Refusing the Romanticism of Identity: Narrative Interventions in Churchill, Benmussa, Duras', in Sue-Ellen Case (ed.), *Performing Feminisms: Feminist Critical Theory and Theatre* (London and Baltimore: Johns Hopkins University Press, 1990), 92–105. Details *Cloud Nine* in context of representation and issues of gender and history.

Fitzsimmons, Linda, 'I won't turn back for you or anyone: Caryl Churchill's Socialist-Feminist Theatre', *Essays in Theatre*, vol. 6, no. 1 (November 1987), 19–29. Examines *Top Girls* and *Fen* as political drama, specifically socialist-feminist drama.

Hanna, Gillian, *Feminism and Theatre*, Theatre Papers, 2nd series, no. 8 (Dartington, Devon: Dartington College, 1978). Discusses Monstrous Regiment's production of *Vinegar Tom*.

Innes, Christopher, 'Caryl Churchill: Theatre as a Model for Change', in *Modern British Drama 1890–1990* (Cambridge: Cambridge University Press, 1992), 460–72. Survey-style essay.

Itzin, Catherine, 'Caryl Churchill', in *Stages in the Revolution* (London: Methuen, 1980), 279–87. Combines brief biographical detail with commentary on early work. Useful detail with regard to *The Legion Hall Bombing* broadcast and the censorship issue.

Keyssar, Helene, 'The Dramas of Caryl Churchill: the Politics of Possibility', in *Feminist Theatre* (Basingstoke: Macmillan, 1984), 77–101. Descriptive chapter on Churchill's plays.

Mairowitz, David Zane, 'God and the Devil', *Plays and Players*, February 1977, 24–5. Review article assessing *Light Shining in Buckinghamshire* and *Vinegar Tom*.

Marohl, Joseph, 'De-realised Women: Performance and Identity in *Top Girls*', *Modern Drama*, vol. 30, no. 3 (September 1987), 376–88. Frames *Top Girls* in context of gender and issues of representation.

Quigley, Austin E., 'Stereotype and Prototype: Character in the Plays of Caryl Churchill', in Enoch Brater (ed.), *Feminine Focus* (Oxford: Oxford University Press, 1989), 25–52. Examines character in context of Churchill's 'social radicalism' and 'theatrical innovation'.

Reinelt, Janelle, 'Beyond Brecht: Britain's New Feminist Drama', in *Performing Feminisms*, 150–9. Has detail on *Vinegar Tom* and Monstrous Regiment.

—— 'Caryl Churchill: Socialist Feminism and Brechtian Dramaturgy', in *After Brecht: British Epic Theater* (Ann Arbor: University of Michigan Press, 1994), 81–107. Excellent study of Churchill as 'one of Brecht's successors'. Teases out complexities and tensions of Brecht and feminism.

Ritchie, Rob (ed.), *The Joint Stock Book: The Making of a Theatre Collective* (London: Methuen, 1987). Has sections on *Light Shining in Buckinghamshire*, *Cloud Nine* and *Fen*.

Sher, Tony, on workshopping *Cloud Nine*, in Ritchie, 138–42.

Solomon, Alisa, 'Witches, Ranters and the Middle Class: The Plays of Caryl Churchill', *Theater*, vol. 12, no. 2 (1981), 49–55. Details *Owners*, *Vinegar Tom* and *Light Shining in Buckinghamshire*.

Stoller, Jennie, on *Fen*, in Ritchie, 150–52.

Swanson, Michael, 'Mother/Daughter Relationships in Three Plays by Caryl Churchill', *Theatre Studies*, 31 (1986), 49–66. Covers *Cloud Nine*, *Top Girls* and *Fen*.

Thomas, Jane, 'The Plays of Caryl Churchill: Essays in Refusal', in Adrian Page (ed.), *The Death of the Playwright?* (Basingstoke: Macmillan, 1992), 160–85. Useful, albeit literary, reading of Churchill through Foucault. Details *Softcops*, *Cloud Nine* and *Top Girls*.

Thurman, Judith, 'The Playwright Who Makes You Laugh About Orgasm, Racism, Class Struggle, Homophobia, Woman-Hating, the British Empire, and the Irrepressible Strangeness of the Human Heart', *Ms.*, May 1982, 51, 54, 57. Surveys Churchill's career and details *Cloud Nine*. Also has interview input from Churchill.

Varty, Anne, 'From Queens to Convicts: Status, Sex and Language in Contemporary British Women's Drama', *Essays and Studies*, 47 (1994), 65–89. Has brief commentary on language and power in *Top Girls* and *Serious Money*.

Wandor, Michelene, 'Free Collective Bargaining', *Time Out*, 30 March–5 April 1979, 14–16. Details workshopping and rehearsal processes of

Cloud Nine.

—— 'Existential Women: *Owners* and *Top Girls'*, in *Look Back in Gender: Sexuality and the Family in Post-War British Drama* (London: Methuen, 1987), 119–25. Brief analysis of domesticity and work in the two plays.

OTHER RELEVANT MATERIAL

Aston, Elaine, *An Introduction to Feminism and Theatre* (London: Routledge, 1995).

—— (ed.), *Feminist Theatre Voices: A Collective Oral History* (Loughborough: Loughborough Theatre Texts, 1997).

Case, Sue-Ellen, *Feminism and Theatre* (Basingstoke: Macmillan, 1988).

—— and Jeanie K. Forte, 'From Formalism to Feminism', *Theater,* 16 (1985), 62–5.

Chesler, Phyllis, *Sacred Bond: Motherhood Under Siege* (London: Virago, 1990).

Cixous, Hélène, 'The Laugh of the Medusa', in Elaine Marks and Isabelle de Courtivron (eds), *New French Feminisms* (Brighton: Harvester, 1981), 245–64.

—— and Catherine Clément, *The Newly Born Woman* (Manchester: Manchester University Press, 1987).

Cohn, Ruby, *Retreats from Realism in Recent English Drama* (Cambridge: Cambridge University Press, 1991).

Diamond, Elin, 'Brechtian Theory / Feminist Theory', *The Drama Review,* vol. 32, no. 1 (Spring 1988), 82–94.

Ellman, Maud, *The Hunger Artists* (London: Virago, 1993).

Faludi, Susan, *Backlash* (London: Vintage, 1991 and 1992).

Grosz, Elizabeth, *Volatile Bodies: Toward a Corporeal Feminism* (Bloomington and Indianapolis: Indiana University Press, 1994).

Hanna, Gillian (compiler), *Monstrous Regiment: A Collective Celebration* (London: Nick Hern, 1991).

Moi, Toril, *Sexual/Textual Politics: Feminist Literary Theory* (London: Routledge, 1985).

Moore, Suzanne, 'New Meanings for New Markets', *Women's Review,* April 1987, 26–7.

Phelan, Peggy, *Unmarked: The Politics of Performance* (London: Routledge, 1993).

Reinelt, Janelle G., and Joseph Roach (eds), *Critical Theory and Performance* (Ann Arbor: University of Michigan Press, 1992).

Showalter, Elaine, *The Female Malady* (London: Virago, 1987).

Index

Smart, Annie, 67
Smith, Ian, 82
Spink, Ian, 81–2, 85, 86, 91–2, 98, 99, 106
Stafford-Clark, Max, 31, 37, 53–5, 70, 90, 104
Taylor, John Russell, 40, 43
Taylor, Paul, 108
Thatcher, Margaret, 38, 75

Thelma and Louise, 52, 87
Thomas, Jane, 63

Wandor, Michelene, 26–7, 31, 65
Wardle, Irving, 51–2, 54–6, 81, 88
Waters, Les, 82
Weir Judith, 96
Whitehouse, Mary, 50–1
Wing-Davey, Mark, 75, 103
Women's Theatre Group, 44

*Recent and
Forthcoming Titles
in the
New Series of*

WRITERS AND
THEIR WORK

*"...this series promises to outshine its own
previously high reputation."*
Times Higher Education Supplement

*"...will build into a fine multi-volume critical
encyclopaedia of English literature."*
Library Review & Reference Review

"...Excellent, informative, readable, and recommended."
NATE News

"...promises to be a rare series of creative scholarship."
Times Educational Supplement

WRITERS AND THEIR WORK

RECENT & FORTHCOMING TITLES

Title	Author
W.H. Auden	Stan Smith
Aphra Behn	Sue Wiseman
A. S. Byatt	Richard Todd
Lord Byron	J. Drummond Bone
Angela Carter	Lorna Sage
Geoffrey Chaucer	Steve Ellis
Children's Literature	Kimberley Reynolds
Caryl Churchill	Elaine Aston
John Clare	John Lucas
Joseph Conrad	Cedric Watts
John Donne	Stevie Davies
Henry Fielding	Jenny Uglow
Elizabeth Gaskell	Kate Flint
William Golding	Kevin McCarron
Graham Greene	Peter Mudford
Hamlet	Ann Thompson & Neil Taylor
Thomas Hardy	Peter Widdowson
David Hare	Jeremy Ridgman
Tony Harrison	Joe Kelleher
William Hazlitt	J.B. Priestley; R.L. Brett (introduction by Michael Foot)
Seamus Heaney	Andrew Murphy
George Herbert	T.S. Eliot (introduction by Peter Porter)
Henry James - The Later Writing	Barbara Hardy
James Joyce	Steven Connor
King Lear	Terence Hawkes
Philip Larkin	Laurence Lerner
Doris Lessing	Elizabeth Maslen
David Lodge	Bernard Bergonzi
Christopher Marlowe	Thomas Healy
Andrew Marvell	Annabel Patterson
Ian McEwan	Kiernan Ryan
A Midsummer Night's Dream	Helen Hackett
Walter Pater	Laurel Brake
Brian Patten	Linda Cookson
Jean Rhys	Helen Carr
Richard II	Margaret Healy
Dorothy Richardson	Carol Watts
Romeo and Juliet	Sasha Roberts
The Sensation Novel	Lyn Pykett
Edmund Spenser	Colin Burrow
J.R.R. Tolkien	Charles Moseley
Leo Tolstoy	John Bayley
Angus Wilson	Peter Conradi
Virginia Woolf	Laura Marcus
Charlotte Yonge	Alethea Hayter